ILLUSTRATED MATTHEW IN GREEK
GlossaHouse Illustrated Biblical Texts

ILLUSTRATED MATTHEW IN GREEK

GlossaHouse Illustrated Biblical Texts

GlossaHouse

Wilmore, KY

www.GlossaHouse.com

Illustrated Matthew in Greek
Copyright © 2022 by GlossaHouse, LLC

All rights reserved. No part of this work may be reproduced or transmitted in any form or by any means, electronic or mechanical, including photocopying and recording, or by means of any information storage or retrieval system, except as may be expressly permitted by the 1976 Copyright Act or in writing from the publisher. Requests for permission should be addressed in writing to the following:

GlossaHouse, LLC
110 Callis Circle
Wilmore, KY 40390

Bible. Matthew. Greek. 2010.
    Illustrated Matthew in Greek : GlossaHouse Illustrated Biblical Texts / Marc Grønbech-Dam, [Keith R. Neely, illustrator].– Wilmore, KY : GlossaHouse, [©2022].
xx, 96 pages : color illustrations ; 28 cm. – (Accessible Greek Resources and Online Studies series. GlossaHouse Illustrated Biblical Texts. Bible)

Summary: The Greek text of the Gospel of Matthew is set within colorful illustrations to represent narration, dialogue, monologue, and scripture quotations, together with a new English version by GlossaHouse translators. Text in English and Koinē Greek.

Library of Congress Control Number: 2022918900

ISBN: 978-1-63663-0311 (pb)

1. Bible. Matthew – Cartoons and comics. I. Grønbech-Dam, Marc II. Neely, Keith R., 1943- III. Translation. IV. Title. V. Series. VI. Bible. Matthew. English. 2022.

SBLGNT is the *The Greek New Testament: SBL Edition*. Copyright 2010 Society of Biblical Literature and Logos Bible Software [ISBN 978-1-58983-535-1]. The SBLGNT text can be found on-line at http://sblgnt.com. Information about the "Society of Biblical Literature" can be found at http://sbl-site.org and "Logos Bible Software" at http://logos.com.

The English translation of Matthew used here is original and has been created by Marc Grønbech-Dam.

The fonts used to create this work are available from linguistsoftware.com/lgku.htm. Illustrations and general illustration layout Copyright © 2006 Neely Publishing LLC.

Cover Design by Fredrick J. Long and T. Michael W. Halcomb
Book Design by Marc Grønbech-Dam.
Illustration Design by Keith R. Neely

AGROS

Accessible Greek Resources and Online Studies

Series Editors

T. Michael W. Halcomb ◆ Fredrick J. Long

AGROS

The Greek word ἀγρός is a field where seeds are planted and growth occurs. It can also denote a small village or community that forms around such a field. The type of community envisioned here is one that attends to Holy Scripture, particularly one that encourages the use of biblical Greek. Accessible Greek Resources and Online Studies (AGROS) is a tiered curriculum suite featuring innovative readers, grammars, specialized studies, and other exegetical resources to encourage and foster the exegetical use of biblical Greek. The goal of AGROS is to facilitate the creation and publication of innovative and affordable print and digital resources for the exposition of Scripture within the context of the global church. The AGROS curriculum includes five tiers, and each tier is indicated on the book's cover: Tier 1 (Beginning I), Tier 2 (Beginning II), Tier 3 (Intermediate I), Tier 4 (Intermediate II), and Tier 5 (Advanced). There are also two resource tracks: Conversational and Translational. Both involve intensive study of morphology, grammar, syntax, and discourse features. The conversational track specifically values the spoken word, and the enhanced learning associated with speaking a language in actual conversation. The translational track values the written word, and encourages analytical study to aide in understanding and translating biblical Greek and other Greek literature. The two resource tracks complement one another and can be pursued independently or together.

GLOSSAHOUSE ILLUSTRATED BIBLICAL TEXTS

TABLE OF CONTENTS

Introduction   xi

ΚΑΤΑ ΙΩΑΝΝΗΝ (According to Matthew)

Κεφ. Α´ (Ch. 1)	1
Κεφ. Β´ (Ch. 2)	2
Κεφ. Γ´ (Ch. 3)	5
Κεφ. Δ´ (Ch. 4)	7
Κεφ. Ε´ (Ch. 5)	10
Κεφ. F´ (Ch. 6)	12
Κεφ. Ζ´ (Ch. 7)	14
Κεφ. Η´ (Ch. 8)	15
Κεφ. Θ´ (Ch. 9)	20
Κεφ. Ι´ (Ch. 10)	24
Κεφ. ΙΑ´ (Ch. 11)	27
Κεφ. ΙΒ´ (Ch. 12)	29
Κεφ. ΙΓ´ (Ch. 13)	34
Κεφ. ΙΔ´ (Ch. 14)	40
Κεφ. ΙΕ´ (Ch. 15)	43
Κεφ. ΙF´ (Ch. 16)	47
Κεφ. ΙΖ´ (Ch. 17)	49
Κεφ. ΙΗ´ (Ch. 18)	52
Κεφ. ΙΘ´ (Ch. 19)	55
Κεφ. Κ´ (Ch. 20)	59
Κεφ. ΚΑ´ (Ch. 21)	61
Κεφ. ΚΒ´ (Ch. 22)	67
Κεφ. ΚΓ´ (Ch. 23)	71
Κεφ. ΚΔ´ (Ch. 24)	74
Κεφ. ΚΕ´ (Ch. 25)	77
Κεφ. ΚF´ (Ch. 26)	80
Κεφ. ΚΖ´ (Ch. 27)	88
Κεφ. ΚΗ´ (Ch. 28)	95

INTRODUCTION

The style and vocabulary of Matthew are often believed to be more sophisticated than Mark. According to Moule, Matthew exhibits a kind of Greek that is less harsh than that of Mark as it uses δέ more often, which improves the Greek along with a greater reluctance to use the historical present, double negatives, and awkward constructions.[1] All these avoidances improve on the Greek of Mark's Gospel.[2] However, Matthew sometimes uses unusual words and constructions. One example of this is his atypical use of the plural βασιλεία τῶν οὐρανῶν "kingdom of (the) heavens" that is likely derived from the Hebrew מלכות השמים.[3] This plural use of οὐρανός reflects a Semitic enhancement of the Greek in Matthew, where heaven is constantly found in the plural and likely carries with it more extensive conceptual and theological nuances.[4] I have tried to retain this stylistic flavor by consistently translating the Greek plural βασιλεία τῶν οὐρανῶν as the English plural "Kingdom of the Heavens."

Another important word in Matthew is μακάριος which famously occurs in the Sermon on the Mount. While it is true that there is "no single, good gloss in English" that denotes the depth and richness of the biblical concept of joyous flourishing to which the word refers, a gloss must nevertheless be provided.[5] In an effort to avoid the seemingly generic "blessed," which might denote a reward for obtaining the states described in the Sermon, or "happy," which seems to reflect a feeling more than a state of being, I have chosen to render μακάριος as "auspicious" in the Sermon on the Mount. The choice of "auspicious" is made deliberately to make the reader aware of the depth and nuance of the concept to which μακάριος refers that might otherwise be overlooked given the profundity of the gloss "blessed" in most English Bible translations.[6] "Auspicious" is furthermore an English gloss that carries a future orientation that meshes well with the future orientation of the makarisms. In other places, like 11:6 and 13:16, I have retained the more traditional gloss "blessed."

Similarly, no single gloss sufficiently covers τέλειος. I have chosen to diverge from the typical English gloss "perfect" because it too readily lends itself to an interpretation of ethical flawlessness which often is not in view in Matthew.[7] Most gloss τέλειος as either "perfect," "complete," or "mature."[8] In an effort to force the reader to wrestle with the depth and nuance of τέλειος, I have chosen to gloss it as "mature" in 5:48 and 19:21 because the context signals a growing into something whole. One should consider the larger context of the Sermon on the Mount, which promotes a righteous growing/maturing amongst Jesus' followers. In this context, a mature follower of Jesus is one who loves his enemies. One should also think

---

[1] C. F. D. Moule, *The Birth of the New Testament*, BNTC, 3rd ed. (London: Adam & Charles Black, 1981), 278–80.

[2] W. D. Davies and Dale C. Allison, *A Critical and Exegetical Commentary on the Gospel According to St. Matthew*, 3 vols. (Edinburgh: T&T Clark, 1988-1997), 1:74.

[3] Jonathan Pennington, *Heaven and Earth in the Gospel of Matthew*, NovTSup 126 (Leiden: Brill, 2007), 104–6.

[4] Ibid., 5.

[5] Jonathan Pennington, *The Sermon on the Mount and Human Flourishing: A Theological Commentary* (Grand Rapids: Baker, 2017), 41.

[6] Ibid., 41-68.

[7] Mogens Müller, *Kommentar til Matthæusevangeliet*, DKNT 3 (Aarhus: Aarhus Universitetsforlag, 2000), 192.

[8] BDAG, s.v. "τέλειος"; E. Yarnold, "Τέλειος in St. Matthew's Gospel," *StEv* 4 (1968): 269–73.

of the νεανίσκος in 19:20, who will only fully mature when he sells everything, gives it to the poor, and then follows Jesus. My translation choice is not meant to indicate that "perfect" is a poor gloss, but I have chosen the gloss "mature" to force readers to ponder the larger meaning(s) of τέλειος.

A few other difficult words to gloss are χρηστός and λεπρός. The word χρηστός occurs only once in Matthew and is consistently translated as "easy." However, several other instances of the word in the NT are glossed as "kind," "good," "beneficial," and so on.[9] Indeed, BDAG lists "useful" or "beneficial" as the two first glosses.[10] Finally, Matthew W. Mitchell suggests χρηστός has been interpreted historically as pointing to the artificial distinction between Jesus and the law-stringent Jews of his time in Matthew's Gospel. Whatever is meant by χρηστός in 11:30, it is quite difficult to see how Jesus's yoke (demand on his followers) is easy.[11] I believe a better and more straightforward translation is to render χρηστός as "good." If the readers decide to interpret χρηστός as carrying the sense of an easy yoke that is perfectly legitimate. However, I do not want to make that interpretive decision for them.

The word λεπρός is often rendered as "leprosy" and subsequently understood to refer to Hansen's disease. However, the term as it occurs in the LXX of Leviticus most often refers to a broad range of skin conditions that render a person ritually impure.[12] Matthew Thiessen cogently argues that the Gospels follow this broad emphasis on various skin conditions vis-à-vis ritual purity rather than leprosy because this disease was unknown in the ancient Mediterranean world until around the third century CE and because when the ancients referred to leprosy, they called it *elephantiasis*.[13] I thus gloss λεπρός as "skin disease" rather than "leprosy."

Other terms that receive special attention in this translation are the words ἀμήν, ῥαββί, and Γαλιλαία. Ἀμήν often references the previous speech or action, which fits well with its use in the Hebrew Scriptures where it regularly affirms what has already been said.[14] This translation thus renders affirmative uses of ἀμήν as "Amen! I am saying to you" rather than the more common gloss "Truly I say to you."

The word ῥαββί can potentially be understood anachronistically since Rabbis, as we know them today, are a later phenomenon. Other issues of the GIBT series have rendered ῥαββί as "My Master" or "Our Master"[15] but I believe the text of Matthew itself makes it clear that ῥαββί is to be understood as "teacher" (23:8) and Judas' choice of ῥαββί in 26:25 is likewise placed in juxtaposition to the other disciples calling Jesus κύριος "lord/master." Rendering ῥαββί as "My Master" therefore presents too many issues and I choose to render ῥαββί as "Rabbi," possible anachronistic interpretations notwithstanding.

---

[9] Luke 5:39; 6:35; Rom 2:4; 1 Cor 15:33; Eph 4:32; 1 Pet 2:3.

[10] BDAG, s.v. "χρηστός."

[11] Matthew W. Mitchell, "The Yoke is Easy, but What of Its Meaning? A Methodological Reflection Masquerading as a Philological Discussion of Matthew 11:30," *JBL* 135 (2016): 321–40.

[12] BDAG, s.v. "λεπρός"

[13] Matthew Thiessen, *Jesus and the Forces of Death: The Gospels' Portrayal of Ritual Impurity within First-Century Judaism* (Grand Rapids: Baker, 2020), 43–68.

[14] T. Michael W. Halcomb and Fredrick J. Long, *Illustrated Mark in Greek*, GlossaHouse Illustrated Biblical Texts (Wilmore, KY: GlossaHouse, 2014), vii; BDAG, s.v. "ἀμήν" §1.a; *HALOT*, s.v. "אמן" §2.

[15] Fredrick J. Long and T. Michael W. Halcomb, *Illustrated John in Greek*, GlossaHouse Illustrated Biblical Texts (Wilmore, KY: GlossaHouse, 2018), xii.

INTRODUCTION

The word Γαλιλαία is translated as "the Galilee" which is in keeping with the historical practice that continues to the present day.[16]

Several other socio-cultural terms such as ἀγορά, πραιτώριον, τάλαντον, δηνάριον, κοδράντην, and γέενναν have been retained via transliteration to preserve a sense of text's *Sitz im Leben*.

Gender inclusiveness is preserved as much as possible, following the advice from Paul Ellingworth to check "male oriented presuppositions" within a translation.[17] As such, the word ἄνθρωπος, when contextually determined not to infer a male necessarily, is rendered as "person" or "people" in the plural.[18] Furthermore, I have chosen to render one particular instance of the plural ἀδελφοί as "siblings" (12:46) rather than the more common "brothers" because it seems that ἀδελφοί can cover both sexes,[19] like *hermanos* in Spanish,[20] if the context warrants. Jesus, in response to the statement that his mother and ἀδελφοί are present, proceeds to mention that whoever does the will of his Father is his ἀδελφός and ἀδελφή and μήτηρ. In light of this inclusive context, one should seriously consider the encompassing nuance of ἀδελφοί in 12:46–49. Similar inclusive meanings of ἀδελφοί in the New Testament are likely in view in Phil 4:1–2, Col 4:15, and 2 Tim 4:21.[21]

12:47 Ἰδοὺ ἡ μήτηρ σου καὶ <u>οἱ ἀδελφοί σου</u> ἔξω ἑστήκασιν, ζητοῦντές σοι λαλῆσαι.
12:47 "Behold your mother and <u>your siblings</u> stand outside, seeking to speak to you"

A similar gender-inclusive stance is taken regarding 21:28, which seeks to render the Greek neuter case in its more neutral, inclusive form. Rather than translating the verse as a man having two sons, which most English translations do, I have decided to follow a small contingent of translators[22] and render the verse as a man having two children, which better reflects the Greek neuter plural τέκνα. That the following verses, by way of definite masculine articles, indicate that the children are male should not force one to alter the neuter case in v. 28.

21:28 A man had <u>two children.</u>
21:28 ἄνθρωπος εἶχεν <u>τέκνα δύο</u>.

Greek word order is followed as much as possible in this translation unless it results in "poor" English. Because of this, a beginning or intermediate student can more readily identify the English glosses with the Greek text. However, δέ usually occurs in the second position yet is most often moved into the first position in the translation.

---

[16] Ibid., xii.
[17] Paul Ellingworth, "The Scope of Inclusive Language," *BT* 43 (1992): 137.
[18] Fredrick J. Long, *Koine Greek Grammar: A Beginning-Intermediate Exegetical and Pragmatic Handbook*, Accessible Greek Resources and Online Studies (Wilmore, KY: GlossaHouse, 2015), 88.
[19] BDAG, s.v. "ἀδελφός" §1.a.
[20] Ellingworth, "Scope of Inclusive Language," 131.
[21] Paul Trebilco, *Self-Designations and Group Identity in the New Testament* (Cambridge: Cambridge University Press, 2012), 24–25.
[22] For example, Edwin K. Broadhead, "An Example of Gender Bias in UBS³," *BT* 40 (1989): 336–37. This gender-neutral translation is also found in Young's literal translation and the Danish translation from 1933 which use the plural form "børn."

Implied words such as *is, it, him, them,* are often provided within brackets […] to provide a good English translation.

> 7:4 καὶ ἰδοὺ ἡ δοκὸς ἐν τῷ ὀφθαλμῷ σοῦ
> 7:4 and behold, the log [is] in your eye
>
> 11:14 καὶ εἰ θέλετε δέξασθαι, αὐτός ἐστιν Ἠλίας ὁ μέλλων ἔρχεσθαι
> 11:14 and if you are willing to accept [it], he is Elijah who is about to come

In Matthew's opening line (called the *incipit*), I have decided to add definite articles in the translation because 1:1 functions as a title for the Gospel and because χριστοῦ, υἱοῦ Δαυὶδ, υἱοῦ Ἀβραάμ function in a titular manner for Jesus.[23] Furthermore, I decided to gloss γενέσεως as "genesis" which is understandable in English and carries the proper allusion to Gen 5:1 in the Septuagint.

> 1:1 Βίβλος γενέσεως Ἰησοῦ χριστοῦ υἱοῦ Δαυὶδ υἱοῦ Ἀβραάμ.
> 1:1 <u>The</u> book of <u>the</u> genesis of Jesus <u>the</u> Messiah <u>the</u> son of David <u>the</u> son of Abraham

Punctuation decisions can be hard to make, and this translation largely follows the SBLGNT except on two occasions where it seems warranted to question those decisions. First, I question the suitability of a question mark in 23:37 as rendered in the SBLGNT:

> 23:37 … ποσάκις ἠθέλησα ἐπισυναγαγεῖν τὰ τέκνα σου, ὃν τρόπον ὄρνις ἐπισυνάγει τὰ νοσσία αὐτῆς ὑπὸ τὰς πτέρυγας, καὶ οὐκ <u>ἠθελήσατε;</u>

Given the inconclusive manuscript evidence for this punctuation choice and the decision to omit the question mark in the NA and UBS editions, as well as the awkwardness of making this verse a question, I have decided to go against the SBLGNT punctuation decision in 23:37.

> 23:37 … how often I wished to gather your children, like a hen gathers her young under the wings, and you <u>did not want to.</u>

Furthermore, I question the SBLGNT decision to omit a question mark when Jesus talks to Judas in 26:50. Jesus's remark can be understood both as an assertion and a question. Following many of the patristic writers and English versions (KJV/RSV/CHSB/YLT), I decided to render it as a question.[24]

> 26:50 ὁ δὲ Ἰησοῦς εἶπεν αὐτῷ· Ἑταῖρε, <u>ἐφ' ὃ πάρει.</u>
> 26:50 But Jesus said to him, "Friend, <u>why are you here?</u>"

I have also inserted exclamation marks every so often to convey the dramatic effect of the Greek narrative itself. Often, this exclamation mark replaces a comma in the SBLGNT.

> 3:7 Γεννήματα ἐχιδνῶν, τίς ὑπέδειξεν ὑμῖν φυγεῖν ἀπὸ τῆς μελλούσης ὀργῆς;
> 3:7 Brood of Vipers! Who showed you to flee from the coming wrath?

---

[23] Even if one does not take Βίβλος γενέσεως to be a title for the whole gospel it still serves as a title of a section thereof.

[24] For more detail see Wesley Olmstead, *Matthew 15–28: A Handbook on the Greek Text*, BHGNT (Waco, TX: Baylor University Press, 2019), 334–35.

INTRODUCTION

5:22 ὃς δ' ἂν εἴπῃ· Μωρέ, ἔνοχος ἔσται εἰς τὴν γέενναν τοῦ πυρός.
5:22 and whoever says, 'You fool!' shall be liable to the Gehenna of fire.

In the below example, the exclamation mark helps the reader see the imperatival force of ἀκουέτω rather than the more permissive flavor in most English versions, which render it "let him hear."

13:43 ὁ ἔχων ὦτα ἀκουέτω.
13:43 The one who has ears, listen!

Note also the insertion of commas around participles used for either slowing down the narrative or giving extra information as well as commas after δέ when translated "so" at the beginning of a sentence.

4:22 οἱ δὲ εὐθέως ἀφέντες τὸ πλοῖον καὶ τὸν πατέρα αὐτῶν ἠκολούθησαν αὐτῷ.
4:22 So they, immediately after leaving the boat and their father, followed him.

Various types of constructions that convey emphasis are translated in different ways. Greek has many ways of indicating prominence in a clause, and the below sample is merely meant to briefly illustrate how I have chosen to deal with some of these constructions.

Superfluous personal pronouns emphasize the subject because verbal endings indicate the subject. These kinds of additional personal pronouns are marked in the translation by adding a reflexive pronoun (*-self*) to the subject.

25:73 Ἀληθῶς καὶ σὺ ἐξ αὐτῶν εἶ
25:73 Truly you yourself are also one of them

Emphatic negation occurs with οὐ μή and is often rendered "certainly not."

5:17 ἰῶτα ἓν ἢ μία κεραία οὐ μὴ παρέλθῃ ἀπὸ τοῦ νόμου.
   one iota or one stroke shall certainly not pass away from the law.

Rhetorical questions that indicate an expected positive or negative answer are indicated as such in the translation and are placed within brackets in italics with an exclamation mark: [*No!/None!*]. Remember the rule of MNOP, which says that μή or μήτι expects a negative answer and οὐ or οὐχί a positive one.

7:9 ἢ τίς ἐστιν ἐξ ὑμῶν ἄνθρωπος, ὃν αἰτήσει ὁ υἱὸς αὐτοῦ ἄρτον — μὴ λίθον ἐπιδώσει αὐτῷ;
7:9 Or which person is there among you, who [when] his son shall ask for bread—shall give him a stone? [*None!*]

7:16 μήτι συλλέγουσιν ἀπὸ ἀκανθῶν ⌜σταφυλὰς ἢ ἀπὸ τριβόλων σῦκα;
7:16 Do [people] collect grapes from thorn bushes or figs from thistles? [*No!*].

Recitative ὅτι sometimes occurs to introduce direct discourse, in which case I have chosen to translate it with the demonstrative pronoun "this" offsetting what follows with a colon (:).

7:23 καὶ τότε ὁμολογήσω αὐτοῖς ὅτι Οὐδέποτε ἔγνων ὑμᾶς·
7:23 And then I shall profess to them this: "I never knew you;"

The verb ἀποκρίνομαι has been glossed in other volumes of the GIBT as *I answer back* to reflect Stephen Levinsohn's suggestion that the verb sometimes indicates an attempt to control the conversation.[25] This volume will follow the same pattern if the context suggests an agonistic setting, i.e., with a challenge and riposte. Consider, for example, one of the Matthean debates between Jesus and his interlocutors in 21:23–24.

> 21:23–24 ... προσῆλθον αὐτῷ διδάσκοντι οἱ ἀρχιερεῖς καὶ οἱ πρεσβύτεροι τοῦ λαοῦ λέγοντες· Ἐν ποίᾳ ἐξουσίᾳ ταῦτα ποιεῖς; καὶ τίς σοι ἔδωκεν τὴν ἐξουσίαν ταύτην; **24** ἀποκριθεὶς δὲ ὁ Ἰησοῦς εἶπεν αὐτοῖς·
>
> 21:23–24 ... the chief priests and elders of the people approached him while teaching saying; "By what authority are you doing these things? And who gave you this authority?" **24** But answering back Jesus said to them;

Conjunctions are always translated in the GHIBT series. Thus, καί and δέ always have a gloss, and many cases of δέ are translated as "so," "now," or "moreover" which helps to make a smoother translation.[26] One example may be seen in 25:37–39.

> 25:37–39 Κύριε, πότε σε εἴδομεν πεινῶντα καὶ ἐθρέψαμεν, ἢ διψῶντα καὶ ἐποτίσαμεν; **38** πότε δέ σε εἴδομεν ξένον καὶ συνηγάγομεν, ἢ γυμνὸν καὶ περιεβάλομεν; **39** πότε δέ σε εἴδομεν ⸀ἀσθενοῦντα ἢ ἐν φυλακῇ καὶ ἤλθομεν πρός σε;
>
> 25:37–39 "Lord, when did we see you hungering and feed [you], or thirsting and give [you] a drink? **38** Additionally, when did we see you a stranger and welcome [you] as a guest, or naked and clothe you? **39** Moreover, when did we see you sick or in prison and come to you?

The reason one can choose various glosses for δέ is that it can be understood as either adversative/contrastive or copulative depending on context.[27] Sometimes understanding δέ as functioning in a copulative or expanding manner, and glossing it as "moreover," will have significant implications. For example, the famous Sermon on Mount has historically and consistently translated the δέ in Jesus' words ἐγὼ δὲ λέγω ὑμῖν in an adversative/contrastive manner. However, the context makes clear that Jesus does not consider his teachings contrastive in every instance. In the Sermon on the Mount, the context often speaks against an adversative/contrastive understanding between Jesus and that which has been heard previously. When that is the case I have glossed δέ as "moreover" to highlight how Jesus sees his teachings to build upon and elaborate on a previous instruction.

> 5:27–28 Ἠκούσατε ὅτι ἐρρέθη· Οὐ μοιχεύσεις. ἐγὼ δὲ λέγω ὑμῖν...
>
> 5:27–28 You heard that it was said; 'You shall not commit adultery.' Moreover, I myself am saying to you...

---

[25] See T. Michael W. Halcomb and Fredrick Long, *Illustrated Mark in Greek*, GlossaHouse Illustrated Biblical Texts (Wilmore, KY: GlossaHouse, 2018), vii; Stephen Levinsohn, *Discourse Features of New Testament Greek: A Coursebook on the Information Structure of New Testament Greek*, 2nd ed. (Dallas: SIL International, 2000), esp. 231–34.

[26] Halcomb and Long, *Illustrated Mark in Greek*, iii.

[27] Robertson argues that δέ is not primarily contrastive/adversative but often refers to a "second comment" or "important addition." For reference, see A. T. Robertson, *Grammar of the Greek New Testament in Light of Historical Research*, 3rd ed. (London: Hodder & Stoughton, 1919), 1184. For similar argumentation about the non-essential contrastive nature of δέ see Levinsohn, *Discourse Features*, 31.

INTRODUCTION   xvii

A contrastive element of δέ does occur in 5:34, 39, and 44 where I have glossed δέ as "but" because the context indicates that Jesus is contrasting his own teaching with something else.

> 5:38–39 Ἠκούσατε ὅτι ἐρρέθη· Ὀφθαλμὸν ἀντὶ ὀφθαλμοῦ καὶ ὀδόντα ἀντὶ ὀδόντος. **39** ἐγὼ <u>δὲ</u> λέγω ὑμῖν μὴ ἀντιστῆναι τῷ πονηρῷ·
> 5:38–39 You heard that it was said, "An eye for an eye and a tooth for a tooth." **39** But I myself am telling you not to resist an evildoer;

Overall, one should heed Stephanie Black who says δέ most often functions in Matthew to generate a sense of change "in participant, a temporal or spatial shift, a move to or from the narrative line, or some other aspect of discontinuity, but these semantic relations are properties of the sentences conjoined by δέ and not δέ itself."[28] The occurrence of δέ does not force a contrastive element in a sentence but might just indicate a shift in speaker. The Sermon on the Mount fits this notion well, switching from what has been said previously to what Jesus is now himself proclaiming. Depending on the context, Jesus's sayings are then sometimes understood as additions and at other times as contrastive.

Verb Tenses in the Indicative Mood are translated rather consistently and conservatively in light of the continuing debates around the Greek verb and verbal aspect. I understand the imperfective verbal aspect to be present in the Present and Imperfect tenses, whereas the perfective aspect occurs in the Aorist tense. Stative or resultative aspects are found in the Perfect and Pluperfect tenses and a future aspect in the Future tense.

<u>Present tense</u> verbs are distinguished by the Historical Present, i.e. in a narrative, or the present tense in direct or indirect discourse. If the present tense is found within direct discourse, it is often translated progressively (i.e. "he is saying"). <u>Historical Present</u> is thus translated as English present and most of the HP in Matthew is found in connection with the verb λέγω, which often introduces some kind of discourse.[29] But as the below example demonstrates, the HP also seems to be employed to create a sense of urgency or vividness in a narrative,[30] or to create a "break in the flow of the discourse" to "highlight an event or speech that follows."[31]

> 2:19 Τελευτήσαντος δὲ τοῦ Ἡρῴδου ἰδοὺ ἄγγελος κυρίου <u>φαίνεται</u> κατ' ὄναρ τῷ Ἰωσὴφ
> 2:19 But after Herod died, behold, an angel of the LORD <u>appears</u> in a dream to Joseph

<u>Imperfect tense</u> verbs are most often translated as a progressive past ("they were saying…") yet there are places where capturing the incompleteness becomes necessary such as in 1:25, 15:22, and 27:23.

> 1:25 καὶ <u>οὐκ ἐγίνωσκεν</u> αὐτὴν ἕως οὗ ἔτεκεν υἱόν·
> 1:25 and <u>he kept on not knowing</u> her until she gave birth to a son;

---

[28] Stephanie L. Black, *Sentence Conjunctions in the Gospel of Matthew: καί, δέ, τότε, γάρ, οὖν, and Asyndeton in Narrative Discourse*, JSNTSup 216 (Sheffield: Sheffield Academic Press, 2002), 174.

[29] Buist M. Fanning, *Verbal Aspect in New Testament Greek*, OTM (Oxford: Clarendon, 1990), 232.

[30] Ibid., 226.

[31] Steven E. Runge, *Discourse Grammar of the Greek New Testament: A Practical Introduction for Teaching and Exegesis* (Peabody, MA: Hendrickson, 2011), 102.

15:22 καὶ ἰδοὺ γυνὴ Χαναναία ἀπὸ τῶν ὁρίων ἐκείνων ἐξελθοῦσα ἔκραζεν λέγουσα·
15:22 And behold a Canaanite woman coming out from those regions kept crying out saying;

27:23 οἱ δὲ περισσῶς ἔκραζον λέγοντες
27:23 But they kept crying out louder saying;

When a change of scenery/setting occurs, the imperfective aspect is sometimes rendered in an inceptive/ingressive manner such as in 5:2 and 13:54.

13:54 καὶ ἐλθὼν εἰς τὴν πατρίδα αὐτοῦ ἐδίδασκεν αὐτοὺς ἐν τῇ συναγωγῇ αὐτῶν
13:54 And having come to his home region he began teaching them in their synagogue

Perfect tense verbs are mostly translated as resultative ("they have gone").[32] In Matthew, the Perfect tense is sometimes employed in the famous fulfillment quotations, which often intrude into the flow of the narrative. The narrative of Matthew is mainly rendered in the Aorist tense, and most English translations render the Perfect γέγονεν as a simple past (Aorist) when it occurs in the fulfillment formulas (1:22; 21:4; 26:56). However, it seems the shift to the Perfect tense might be a deliberate choice signaling to the reader an important summary interjection by a narrator, almost like the chorus from ancient Greek literature.[33] I have thus chosen to highlight the resultative aspect of the Perfect tense in those fulfillment quotations.

1:22 τοῦτο δὲ ὅλον γέγονεν ἵνα …
1:22 Now all this has happened in order …

Future tense verbs are rendered as simple futures ("he shall say") unless otherwise needed.

Aorist tense verbs are most often translated as simple past ("he said").

Pluperfect tense verbs are translated as resultative in past time ("they had gone"), except when context dictates a differently as in 13:2 where it seems to best fit a simple past.

Non-Indicative Mood verbs have been rendered consistently, as much as possible, in order to promote observation and conversation. The Perfect tense is rendered in a stative/resultative aspect, the Present tense in an imperfective/progressive aspect, and the Aorist tense in a perfective/completed aspect.

For participles, which are tricky to translate, I have generally translated pre-nuclear verbal participles in the Present tense as contemporaneous ("while/as going") and the Aorist tense as antecedent or time prior ("after going/having gone"). However, if the Aorist participle is related to an Aorist main verb, it is sometimes rendered as contemporaneous. Post-nuclear verbal participles are rendered as simple participles ("seeing, walking," etc.) when they further describe the main verb. However, the reader of Matthew should carefully consider how Greek participles can function in various constructions and that participles should

---

[32] It should be noted that the Perfect can also refer to a "concurrent state." See Robert Samuel David Crellin, *The Syntax and Semantics of the Perfect Active in Literary Koine Greek*, Publications of the Philological Society 47 (Chichester: Wiley-Blackwell, 2016), 1.

[33] Nicholas G. Piotrowski, *Matthew's New David at the End of Exile: A Socio-rhetorical Study of Scriptural Quotations*, NovTSup 170 (Leiden: Brill, 2016), 41.

be translated based on context. This means one must allow for a variety of acceptable translations,[34] especially for the procedural use, traditionally called "attendant circumstance/circumstantial."[35]

Pre-nuclear participles (also known as attendant/circumstantial) that are not adverbial or temporally prior but still occur right before the main verb function to set off the nuclear verb and perhaps continue a theme or add gravitas to the event. This kind of thinking affects how I have decided to translate pre-nuclear participles that occur before imperatives.

Most English translations of 28:19 render the Greek in a way that might lead one to think the Greek clause consists of two imperatives divided by the conjunction "and."[36] In taking a more literal approach, others see the first aorist participle as giving some background information, i.e. "having-gone, therefore, make disciples of all nations."[37] In an effort to avoid rendering the English translation in a way that might lead one to think the Greek clause consists of two imperatives divided by "and,"[38] and to avoid a disassociation between the participle and the imperative, I have chosen a slightly different approach. This is because we must show that the Greek indicates the first participle ranks below the main verb. Kathleen Callow argues that the "effect" is more prominent to the "cause," and the goal is more than the means.[39]
I have thus chosen to translate 28:19 as follows:

28:19 πορευθέντες οὖν μαθητεύσατε
28:19 Go, therefore, to make disciples

In my English translation, I hope that the "go to" creates a sense of subordination, although the imperative becomes more like an infinitive. However, the clause as a whole retains an imperatival aspect. So, the translation of 28:19 "go, therefore, to make disciples" retains the prominence of the imperative by making it purposive. I realize that the difference between the above translation and that of most English Bibles is the difference between "and" and "to." However, it seems this proposed translation choice might help readers see the prominence of the imperative and avoid thinking the "and" might link two Greek imperatives. Matthew does have similar constructions where two imperatives are linked by "and" (5:12, 29, 30, 15:10, 16:6, 18:8, 9), which English translations render the same as 28:19 where a participle and imperative are linked

---

[34] Fredrick J. Long, *Koine Greek Grammar: A Beginning-Intermediate Exegetical and Pragmatic Handbook*, Accessible Greek Resources and Online Studies (Wilmore, KY: GlossaHouse, 2015), 349–50.

[35] Long, *Koine Greek Grammar*, 326–51.

[36] Most English translations take this route by rendering the pertinent participles as finite verbs and linking them to the main verb by using "and." This is likely because these translations share Wallace's notion that the participle takes on the imperatival force or "mood" from the main verb which is why 28:19 is called the Great Commission and not the "Great Suggestion." For reference, see Daniel B. Wallace, *Greek Grammar Beyond the Basics: An Exegetical Syntax of the New Testament* (Grand Rapids: Zondervan, 1996), 644–45.

[37] Randall Buth, "Participles as Pragmatic Choice: Where Semantics Meet Pragmatics," in *The Greek Verb Revisited: A Fresh Approach for Biblical Exegesis*, eds. Steven Runge & Christopher Fresch (Bellingham, WA: Lexham, 2016), 280–81.

[38] Most English translations take this route by rendering the pertinent participles as finite verbs and linking them to the main verb by using "and." This is likely because these translations share Wallace's notion that the participle takes on the imperatival force or "mood" from the main verb which is why 28:19 is called the Great Commission and not the "Great Suggestion." See Wallace, *Greek Grammar Beyond the Basics*, 644–45.

[39] Kathleen Callow, *Man and Message: A Guide to Meaning-Based Text Analysis* (Lanham, MD: Summer Institute of Linguistics; University Press of America, 1998), 156.

by the English "and." However, since these are two different kinds of constructions in Greek, I believe an English translation should make it easier for the reader to see the difference.

Other examples of my translational choice in 28:19 are listed below. Note that most of the examples occur with a participial form of πορεύομαι immediately before the nuclear verbal imperative. Going is thus a necessary part of the command and carries an imperatival aspect, yet it is grammatically subordinate to the imperative.

2:8 Πορευθέντες ἐξετάσατε ἀκριβῶς περὶ τοῦ παιδίου
2:8 Go to search carefully for the child!

2:13 ἐγερθεὶς παράλαβε τὸ παιδίον
2:13 Get up to take the child

9:13 πορευθέντες δὲ μάθετε τί ἐστιν·
9:13 Now go to learn what this means;

9:18 ἀλλὰ ἐλθὼν ἐπίθες τὴν χεῖρά σου ἐπ' αὐτήν
9:18 But go to put your hand on her

10:7 πορευόμενοι δὲ κηρύσσετε λέγοντες ὅτι
10:7 Now go to preach saying this

11:4 πορευθέντες ἀπαγγείλατε Ἰωάννῃ
11:4 Go to announce to John

17:27 πορευθεὶς εἰς θάλασσαν βάλε ἄγκιστρον
17:27 go to the sea to cast a fishhook

ΚΑΤΑ ΜΑΘΘΑΙΟΝ

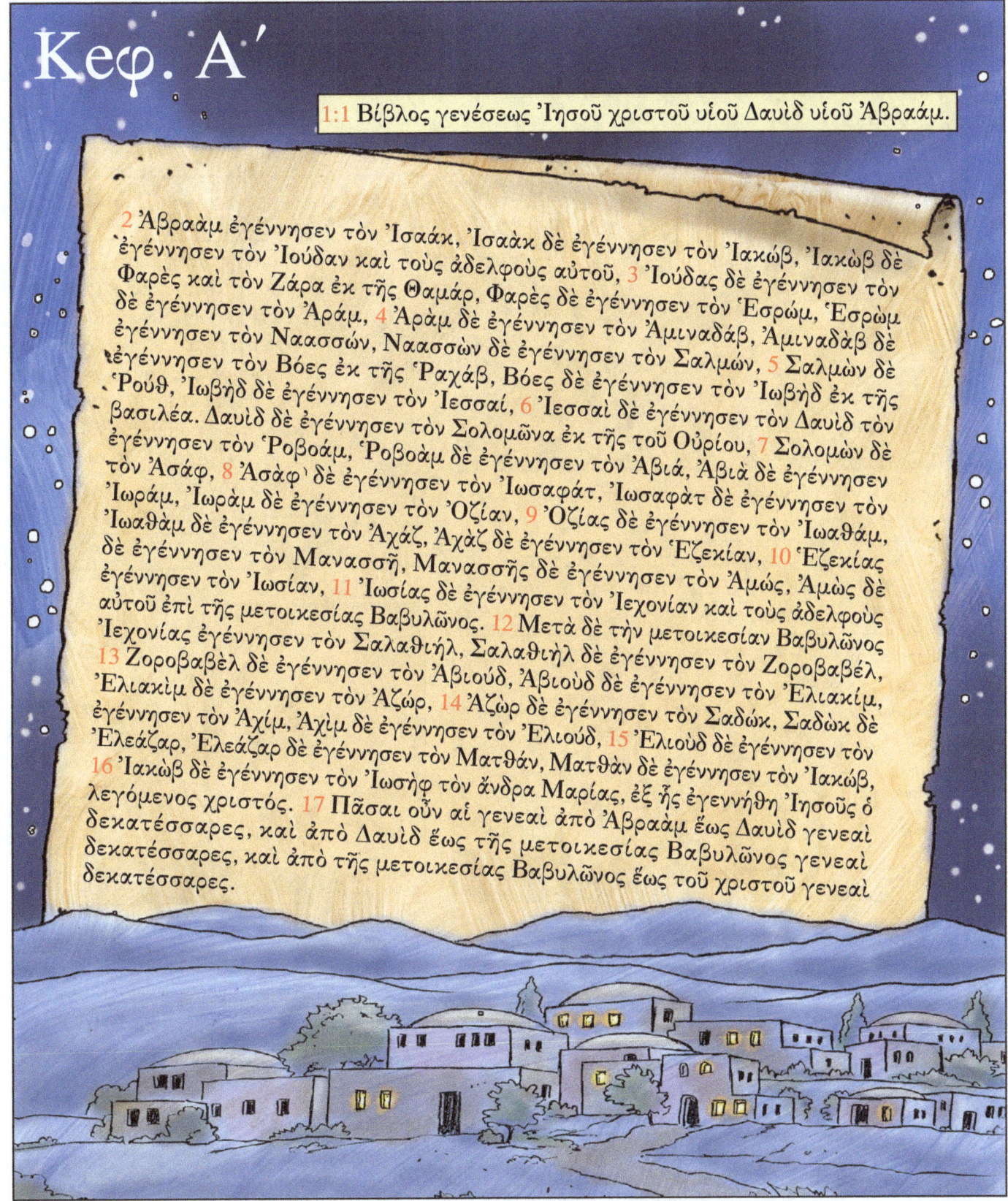

1:1 The book of the genesis of Jesus the Messiah the son of David the son of Abraham. 2 Abraham begat Isaac, and Isaac begat Jacob, and Jacob begat Judah and his brothers, 3 and Judah begat Phares and Zara from Tamar, and Phares begat Esrom, and Esrom Aram, 4 and Aram begat Aminadab, and Aminadab begat Naasson, and Naasson begat Salmon, 5 and Salmon begat Boaz from Rahab, and Boaz begat Obed from Ruth, and Obed begat Jesse, 6 and Jesse begat David the King. Now David begat Solomon from the wife of Uriah, 7 and Solomon begat Jeroboam, and Jeroboam begat Abijah, and Abijah begat Asa, 8 and Asa begat Josaphat, and Josaphat begat Jehoram, and Jehoram begat Uzziah, 9 and Uzziah begat Jotham, and Jotham begat Ahaz, and Ahaz begat Hezekiah, 10 and Hezekiah begat Manasseh, and Menasseh begat Amon, and Amon begat Josiah, 11 and Josiah begat Jeconiah and his brothers at the time of the Babylonian exile. 12 Now after the Babylonian exile Jeconiah begat Shealtiel, and Shealtiel begat Zerubbabel, 13 and Zerubbabel begat Abiud, and Abiud begat Eliakim, and Eliakim begat Azor, 14 and Azor begat Zadok, and Zadok begat Akim, and Akim begat Eliud, 15 and Eliud begat Eleazar, and Eleazar begat Matthan, and Matthan begat Jacob, 16 and Jacob begat Joseph the husband of Mary, from whom was born Jesus who is called "Messiah." 17 Now all the generations from Abraham until David are fourteen generations, and from David until the Babylonian exile fourteen generations, and from the Babylonian exile until the Messiah fourteen generations.

Matthew 1:18-2:2

18 Τοῦ δὲ Ἰησοῦ χριστοῦ ἡ γένεσις οὕτως ἦν. μνηστευθείσης τῆς μητρὸς αὐτοῦ Μαρίας τῷ Ἰωσήφ, πρὶν ἢ συνελθεῖν αὐτοὺς εὑρέθη ἐν γαστρὶ ἔχουσα ἐκ πνεύματος ἁγίου. 19 Ἰωσὴφ δὲ ὁ ἀνὴρ αὐτῆς, δίκαιος ὢν καὶ μὴ θέλων αὐτὴν δειγματίσαι, ἐβουλήθη λάθρα ἀπολῦσαι αὐτήν. 20 ταῦτα δὲ αὐτοῦ ἐνθυμηθέντος ἰδοὺ ἄγγελος κυρίου κατ᾽ ὄναρ ἐφάνη αὐτῷ λέγων·

Ἰωσὴφ υἱὸς Δαυίδ, μὴ φοβηθῇς παραλαβεῖν Μαρίαν τὴν γυναῖκά σου, τὸ γὰρ ἐν αὐτῇ γεννηθὲν ἐκ πνεύματός ἐστιν ἁγίου· 21 τέξεται δὲ υἱὸν καὶ καλέσεις τὸ ὄνομα αὐτοῦ Ἰησοῦν, αὐτὸς γὰρ σώσει τὸν λαὸν αὐτοῦ ἀπὸ τῶν ἁμαρτιῶν αὐτῶν

22 τοῦτο δὲ ὅλον γέγονεν ἵνα πληρωθῇ τὸ ῥηθὲν ὑπὸ κυρίου διὰ τοῦ προφήτου λέγοντος·

23 Ἰδοὺ ἡ παρθένος ἐν γαστρὶ ἕξει καὶ τέξεται υἱόν, καὶ καλέσουσιν τὸ ὄνομα αὐτοῦ Ἐμμανουήλ· ὅ ἐστιν μεθερμηνευόμενον Μεθ᾽ ἡμῶν ὁ θεός.

24 ἐγερθεὶς δὲ ὁ Ἰωσὴφ ἀπὸ τοῦ ὕπνου ἐποίησεν ὡς προσέταξεν αὐτῷ

ὁ ἄγγελος κυρίου καὶ παρέλαβεν τὴν γυναῖκα αὐτοῦ· 25 καὶ οὐκ ἐγίνωσκεν αὐτὴν ἕως οὗ ἔτεκεν υἱόν· καὶ ἐκάλεσεν τὸ ὄνομα αὐτοῦ Ἰησοῦν.

Κεφ. Β´

2.1 Τοῦ δὲ Ἰησοῦ γεννηθέντος ἐν Βηθλέεμ τῆς Ἰουδαίας ἐν ἡμέραις Ἡρῴδου τοῦ βασιλέως, ἰδοὺ μάγοι ἀπὸ ἀνατολῶν παρεγένοντο εἰς Ἱεροσόλυμα 2 λέγοντες·

Ποῦ ἐστιν ὁ τεχθεὶς βασιλεὺς τῶν Ἰουδαίων; εἴδομεν γὰρ αὐτοῦ τὸν ἀστέρα ἐν τῇ ἀνατολῇ καὶ ἤλθομεν προσκυνῆσαι αὐτῷ.

18 Now the genesis of Jesus the Messiah was as follows: after his mother Mary betrothed to Joseph, before they came together, she was found to be pregnant by the Holy Spirit. 19 Now Joseph her husband, being righteous and not wishing to publicly expose her, determined to divorce her secretly. 20 But while considering these things, behold, an angel of the LORD appeared in a dream saying, "Joseph son of David, do not be afraid to take Mary as your wife, for that which was conceived in her is from the Holy Spirit. 21 So she shall give birth to a son and you shall call him Jesus, for he himself will save his people from their sins." 22 Now all this has happened in order that what was spoken by the LORD through the prophet would be fulfilled saying, 23 "Behold! The virgin will be pregnant and will give birth to a son, and they shall call his name Immanuel; which means 'God with us.'" 24 Having risen from the sleep Joseph did as the angel of the LORD commanded and took his wife; 25 and he kept on not knowing her until she gave birth to a son; and he called his name Jesus. 2:1 Now after Jesus was born in Bethlehem of Judah in the days of Herod the king, behold! Magi from the East arrived in Jerusalem 2 saying, "Where is the one born king of the Jews? For we observed his star at its rising and we came to pay homage to him."

Matthew 2:3-15

³ ἀκούσας δὲ ὁ βασιλεὺς Ἡρῴδης ἐταράχθη καὶ πᾶσα Ἱεροσόλυμα μετ' αὐτοῦ, ⁴ καὶ συναγαγὼν πάντας τοὺς ἀρχιερεῖς καὶ γραμματεῖς τοῦ λαοῦ ἐπυνθάνετο παρ' αὐτῶν ποῦ ὁ χριστὸς γεννᾶται. ⁵ οἱ δὲ εἶπαν αὐτῷ·

Ἐν Βηθλέεμ τῆς Ἰουδαίας· οὕτως γὰρ γέγραπται διὰ τοῦ προφήτου· ⁶ Καὶ σύ, Βηθλέεμ γῆ Ἰούδα, οὐδαμῶς ἐλαχίστη εἶ ἐν τοῖς ἡγεμόσιν Ἰούδα· ἐκ σοῦ γὰρ ἐξελεύσεται ἡγούμενος, ὅστις ποιμανεῖ τὸν λαόν μου τὸν Ἰσραήλ.

Πορευθέντες ἐξετάσατε ἀκριβῶς περὶ τοῦ παιδίου· ἐπὰν δὲ εὕρητε, ἀπαγγείλατέ μοι, ὅπως κἀγὼ ἐλθὼν προσκυνήσω αὐτῷ.

⁷ Τότε Ἡρῴδης λάθρα καλέσας τοὺς μάγους ἠκρίβωσεν παρ' αὐτῶν τὸν χρόνον τοῦ φαινομένου ἀστέρος, ⁸ καὶ πέμψας αὐτοὺς εἰς Βηθλέεμ εἶπεν·

¹¹ καὶ ἐλθόντες εἰς τὴν οἰκίαν εἶδον τὸ παιδίον μετὰ Μαρίας τῆς μητρὸς αὐτοῦ, καὶ πεσόντες προσεκύνησαν αὐτῷ, καὶ ἀνοίξαντες τοὺς θησαυροὺς αὐτῶν προσήνεγκαν αὐτῷ δῶρα, χρυσὸν καὶ λίβανον καὶ σμύρναν. ¹² καὶ χρηματισθέντες κατ' ὄναρ μὴ ἀνακάμψαι πρὸς Ἡρῴδην δι' ἄλλης ὁδοῦ ἀνεχώρησαν εἰς τὴν χώραν αὐτῶν.

⁹ οἱ δὲ ἀκούσαντες τοῦ βασιλέως ἐπορεύθησαν, καὶ ἰδοὺ ὁ ἀστὴρ ὃν εἶδον ἐν τῇ ἀνατολῇ προῆγεν αὐτούς, ἕως ἐλθὼν ἐστάθη ἐπάνω οὗ ἦν τὸ παιδίον. ¹⁰ ἰδόντες δὲ τὸν ἀστέρα ἐχάρησαν χαρὰν μεγάλην σφόδρα.

¹⁴ ὁ δὲ ἐγερθεὶς παρέλαβε τὸ παιδίον καὶ τὴν μητέρα αὐτοῦ νυκτὸς καὶ ἀνεχώρησεν εἰς Αἴγυπτον, ¹⁵ καὶ ἦν ἐκεῖ ἕως τῆς τελευτῆς Ἡρῴδου· ἵνα πληρωθῇ τὸ ῥηθὲν ὑπὸ κυρίου διὰ τοῦ προφήτου λέγοντος·

Ἐξ Αἰγύπτου ἐκάλεσα τὸν υἱόν μου.

¹³ Ἀναχωρησάντων δὲ αὐτῶν ἰδοὺ ἄγγελος κυρίου φαίνεται κατ' ὄναρ τῷ Ἰωσὴφ λέγων·

Ἐγερθεὶς παράλαβε τὸ παιδίον καὶ τὴν μητέρα αὐτοῦ καὶ φεῦγε εἰς Αἴγυπτον, καὶ ἴσθι ἐκεῖ ἕως ἂν εἴπω σοι· μέλλει γὰρ Ἡρῴδης ζητεῖν τὸ παιδίον τοῦ ἀπολέσαι αὐτό.

³ But, King Herod having heard [this], was disturbed and all of Jerusalem with him, ⁴ and having gathered all the high priests and scribes of the people, he was inquiring of them where the Messiah was to be born. ⁵ So they said to him, "In Bethlehem of Judea. For thus it has been written through the prophet: ⁶ 'And you, Bethlehem in the land of Judah, are certainly not least among the rulers of Judah. For from you will come a ruler who will shepherd my people Israel.'" ⁷ Then Herod, secretly having called the Magi, ascertained from them the time of the star's appearance, ⁸ and sending them to Bethlehem he said, "Go to search carefully for the child; now when you find him, inform me, so that I too, coming, might pay homage to him." ⁹ So, after hearing the king, they went, and behold the star, which they saw in the East, was going before them until, having come, it stood above where the child was. ¹⁰ And after seeing the star, they rejoiced greatly with much joy. ¹¹ And coming into the house they saw the child with Mary his mother. And falling down they paid homage to him, and having opened their treasure chests they offered him gifts of gold, frankincense, and myrrh. ¹² And after being warned in a dream not to return to Herod they left to their country through another route. ¹³ But having taken refuge, behold, an angel of the LORD appears to Joseph in a dream saying, "Get up to take the child and his mother and flee to Egypt, and remain there until I tell you. For Herod is about to search for the child to destroy it." ¹⁴ So getting up, he took the child and his mother in the night and withdrew to Egypt, ¹⁵ and he was there until Herod died; in order that what was spoken by the LORD through the prophet would be fulfilled saying, "Out of Egypt I called my son."

Matthew 2:16-23

16 Τότε Ἡρῴδης ἰδὼν ὅτι ἐνεπαίχθη ὑπὸ τῶν μάγων ἐθυμώθη λίαν, καὶ ἀποστείλας ἀνεῖλεν πάντας τοὺς παῖδας τοὺς ἐν Βηθλέεμ καὶ ἐν πᾶσι τοῖς ὁρίοις αὐτῆς ἀπὸ διετοῦς καὶ κατωτέρω, κατὰ τὸν χρόνον ὃν ἠκρίβωσεν παρὰ τῶν μάγων.

17 τότε ἐπληρώθη τὸ ῥηθὲν διὰ Ἰερεμίου τοῦ προφήτου λέγοντος·

18 Φωνὴ ἐν Ῥαμὰ ἠκούσθη, κλαυθμὸς καὶ ὀδυρμὸς πολύς· Ῥαχὴλ κλαίουσα τὰ τέκνα αὐτῆς, καὶ οὐκ ἤθελεν παρακληθῆναι ὅτι οὐκ εἰσίν.

19 Τελευτήσαντος δὲ τοῦ Ἡρῴδου ἰδοὺ ἄγγελος κυρίου φαίνεται κατ᾽ ὄναρ τῷ Ἰωσὴφ ἐν Αἰγύπτῳ 20 λέγων·

Ἐγερθεὶς παράλαβε τὸ παιδίον καὶ τὴν μητέρα αὐτοῦ καὶ πορεύου εἰς γῆν Ἰσραήλ, τεθνήκασιν γὰρ οἱ ζητοῦντες τὴν ψυχὴν τοῦ παιδίου.

21 ὁ δὲ ἐγερθεὶς παρέλαβεν τὸ παιδίον καὶ τὴν μητέρα αὐτοῦ καὶ εἰσῆλθεν εἰς γῆν Ἰσραήλ. 22 ἀκούσας δὲ ὅτι Ἀρχέλαος βασιλεύει τῆς Ἰουδαίας ἀντὶ τοῦ πατρὸς αὐτοῦ Ἡρῴδου ἐφοβήθη ἐκεῖ ἀπελθεῖν·

χρηματισθεὶς δὲ κατ᾽ ὄναρ ἀνεχώρησεν εἰς τὰ μέρη τῆς Γαλιλαίας, 23 καὶ ἐλθὼν κατῴκησεν εἰς πόλιν λεγομένην Ναζαρέτ, ὅπως πληρωθῇ τὸ ῥηθὲν διὰ τῶν προφητῶν ὅτι

5:1 Ναζωραῖος κληθήσεται.

[16] Then Herod, after seeing that he was tricked by the Magi, became furious, and having sent out [order/soldiers], he killed all the children in Bethlehem and in all its regions from the age of two or younger, according to the time he ascertained from the Magi. [17] Then was fulfilled that which was spoken through Jeremiah the prophet; [18] "A voice was heard in Ramah, weeping and great mourning! Rachel weeping for her children, and she was not wanting to be comforted because they are not [alive]." [19] Now after Herod died, behold, an angel of the LORD appears to Joseph in a dream in Egypt [20] saying, "Get up to take the child and his mother and go to the land of Israel, for the ones who were seeking the life of the child have died." [21] So, after getting up, he took the child and his mother, and entered into the land of Israel. [22] But having heard that Archelaos ruled Judea in place of his father, Herod, he was afraid to return there. Moreover, having been warned in a dream, he withdrew to the region of the Galilee, [23] and after arriving he settled down in a town called Nazareth in order that what was spoken through the prophets would be fulfilled [saying] this: "He shall be called a Nazorean."

Matthew 3:1-6

3:1 Now in those days John the Baptist comes preaching in the wilderness of Judea ² and saying, "Repent! For the Kingdom of the Heavens has come near." ³ For this is the one spoken about through Isaiah the prophet saying: "A voice crying in the wilderness. Prepare the way of the LORD make straight his paths." ⁴ Now John himself was wearing a garment from camel's hairs and a leather belt around his waist, and his food was locusts and wild honey. ⁵ Then Jerusalem was going out toward him and all of Judea and the whole district of Jordan, ⁶ and they were being baptized in the Jordan River by him confessing their sins.

Matthew 3:7-17

7 Ἰδὼν δὲ πολλοὺς τῶν Φαρισαίων καὶ Σαδδουκαίων ἐρχομένους ἐπὶ τὸ βάπτισμα αὐτοῦ εἶπεν αὐτοῖς·

Γεννήματα ἐχιδνῶν, τίς ὑπέδειξεν ὑμῖν φυγεῖν ἀπὸ τῆς μελλούσης ὀργῆς; 8 ποιήσατε οὖν καρπὸν ἄξιον τῆς μετανοίας 9 καὶ μὴ δόξητε λέγειν ἐν ἑαυτοῖς· Πατέρα ἔχομεν τὸν Ἀβραάμ, λέγω γὰρ ὑμῖν ὅτι δύναται ὁ θεὸς ἐκ τῶν λίθων τούτων ἐγεῖραι τέκνα τῷ Ἀβραάμ

10 ἤδη δὲ ἡ ἀξίνη πρὸς τὴν ῥίζαν τῶν δένδρων κεῖται· πᾶν οὖν δένδρον μὴ ποιοῦν καρπὸν καλὸν ἐκκόπτεται καὶ εἰς πῦρ βάλλεται. 11 Ἐγὼ μὲν ὑμᾶς βαπτίζω ἐν ὕδατι εἰς μετάνοιαν· ὁ δὲ ὀπίσω μου ἐρχόμενος ἰσχυρότερός μού ἐστιν, οὗ οὐκ εἰμὶ ἱκανὸς τὰ ὑποδήματα βαστάσαι· αὐτὸς ὑμᾶς βαπτίσει ἐν πνεύματι ἁγίῳ καὶ πυρί· 12 οὗ τὸ πτύον ἐν τῇ χειρὶ αὐτοῦ, καὶ διακαθαριεῖ τὴν ἅλωνα αὐτοῦ καὶ συνάξει τὸν σῖτον αὐτοῦ εἰς τὴν ἀποθήκην, τὸ δὲ ἄχυρον κατακαύσει πυρὶ ἀσβέστῳ.

13 Τότε παραγίνεται ὁ Ἰησοῦς ἀπὸ τῆς Γαλιλαίας ἐπὶ τὸν Ἰορδάνην πρὸς τὸν Ἰωάννην τοῦ βαπτισθῆναι ὑπ' αὐτοῦ. 14 ὁ δὲ Ἰωάννης διεκώλυεν αὐτὸν λέγων·

15 ἀποκριθεὶς δὲ ὁ Ἰησοῦς εἶπεν πρὸς αὐτόν·

Ἐγὼ χρείαν ἔχω ὑπὸ σοῦ βαπτισθῆναι, καὶ σὺ ἔρχῃ πρός με;

Ἄφες ἄρτι, οὕτως γὰρ πρέπον ἐστὶν ἡμῖν πληρῶσαι πᾶσαν δικαιοσύνην.

τότε ἀφίησιν αὐτόν.

16 βαπτισθεὶς δὲ ὁ Ἰησοῦς εὐθὺς ἀνέβη ἀπὸ τοῦ ὕδατος· καὶ ἰδοὺ ἠνεῴχθησαν οἱ οὐρανοί, καὶ εἶδεν πνεῦμα θεοῦ καταβαῖνον ὡσεὶ περιστερὰν ἐρχόμενον ἐπ' αὐτόν·

17 καὶ ἰδοὺ φωνὴ ἐκ τῶν οὐρανῶν λέγουσα·

Οὗτός ἐστιν ὁ υἱός μου ὁ ἀγαπητός, ἐν ᾧ εὐδόκησα.

---

7 Now after seeing many of the Pharisees and Sadducees coming to his baptism he said to them, "Brood of Vipers! Who showed you to flee from the coming wrath? 8 Then produce fruit worthy of repentance 9 and do not think to say amongst yourselves, 'We have Abraham as our father,' for I am saying to you this: 'God is able from these stones to raise up children of Abraham.' 10 But already the axe is laid by the root of the trees; so each tree that is not producing a good fruit is being cut down and cast into the fire. 11 I myself baptize you with water for repentance; but the one who is coming after me is stronger than I, his sandals I am not able to carry; he shall baptize you in [the] Holy Spirit and fire; 12 his winnowing fork in his hand, and he shall clean out his threshing floor and he shall gather his wheat into the storehouse, but the chaff he shall burn with unquenchable fire." 13 Then Jesus comes from the Galilee to the Jordan to John to be baptized by him. 14 But John was preventing him saying, "I myself have a need to be baptized by you, and you yourself are coming to me?" 15 But answering back, Jesus said to him, "Let it be so now, for thus it is proper for us to fulfill all righteousness." Then he permits him. 16 Now after being baptized, Jesus immediately arose out of the water; and behold the heavens were opened, and he saw God's Spirit descending as a dove coming on him. 17 And behold a voice from the heavens saying, "This is my beloved son, with whom I am pleased."

Matthew 4:1-11

[1] Then Jesus was led into the wilderness by the Spirit, to be tempted by the devil. [2] And after fasting 40 days and 40 nights he was hungry. [3] And, approaching, the tempter said to him, "If you are the Son of God, speak that these stones would become bread." [4] But answering back he said, "It has been written, 'Humankind shall not live on bread alone, but on each word going out through God's mouth.'" [5] Then the devil takes him into the holy city, and places him on the pinnacle of the Temple, [6] and says to him, "If you are the Son of God, throw yourself down; for it has been written [like] this: 'For He shall command His angels concerning you and in their hands they shall lift you up, so that you will not strike your foot against a stone.'" [7] Jesus said to him, "Again it has been written, 'You shall not test the Lord your God.'" [8] Again the devil takes him to a very high mountain and shows him all the kingdoms of the world and their glory [9] and said to him, "I shall give you all of these things, if, falling down, you worship me." [10] Then Jesus says to him, "Leave, Satan, for it has been written, 'The Lord your God you shall worship and him alone you shall serve.'" [11] Then the devil leaves him, and behold angels came and they were ministering to him.

Matthew 4:12-17

12 But hearing that John was handed over he withdrew into the Galilee. 13 And having left Nazareth, coming, he dwelled in Capernaum-by-the-sea in the regions of Zebulun and Naphtali, 14 so that which was spoken through Isaiah the prophet would be fulfilled saying, 15 "Land of Zebulun and land of Naphtali, way of the sea, beyond the Jordan, Galilee of the Gentiles, 16 the people who sit in darkness saw a great light, and those sitting in the region and [in the] shadow of death a light arose for them." 17 From then on Jesus began to preach and to say, "Repent! For the Kingdom of the Heavens has come near."

Matthew 5:1-12

Κεφ. Ε′

5:1 Ἰδὼν δὲ τοὺς ὄχλους ἀνέβη εἰς τὸ ὄρος· καὶ καθίσαντος αὐτοῦ προσῆλθαν αὐτῷ οἱ μαθηταὶ αὐτοῦ· 2 καὶ ἀνοίξας τὸ στόμα αὐτοῦ ἐδίδασκεν αὐτοὺς λέγων·

3 Μακάριοι οἱ πτωχοὶ τῷ πνεύματι, ὅτι αὐτῶν ἐστιν ἡ βασιλεία τῶν οὐρανῶν. 4 μακάριοι οἱ πενθοῦντες, ὅτι αὐτοὶ παρακληθήσονται. 5 μακάριοι οἱ πραεῖς, ὅτι αὐτοὶ κληρονομήσουσι τὴν γῆν. 6 μακάριοι οἱ πεινῶντες καὶ διψῶντες τὴν δικαιοσύνην, ὅτι αὐτοὶ χορτασθήσονται. 7 μακάριοι οἱ ἐλεήμονες, ὅτι αὐτοὶ ἐλεηθήσονται. 8 μακάριοι οἱ καθαροὶ τῇ καρδίᾳ, ὅτι αὐτοὶ τὸν θεὸν ὄψονται. 9 μακάριοι οἱ εἰρηνοποιοί, ὅτι αὐτοὶ υἱοὶ θεοῦ κληθήσονται. 10 μακάριοι οἱ δεδιωγμένοι ἕνεκεν δικαιοσύνης, ὅτι αὐτῶν ἐστιν ἡ βασιλεία τῶν οὐρανῶν. 11 μακάριοί ἐστε ὅταν ὀνειδίσωσιν ὑμᾶς καὶ διώξωσιν καὶ εἴπωσιν πᾶν πονηρὸν καθ᾽ ὑμῶν ψευδόμενοι ἕνεκεν ἐμοῦ. 12 χαίρετε καὶ ἀγαλλιᾶσθε, ὅτι ὁ μισθὸς ὑμῶν πολὺς ἐν τοῖς οὐρανοῖς· οὕτως γὰρ ἐδίωξαν τοὺς προφήτας τοὺς πρὸ ὑμῶν.

5:1 Now seeing the crowds he ascended up the mountain; and sitting down his disciples came to him; 2 and opening his mouth he began teaching them saying, 3 "Auspicious are the poor in spirit, for theirs is the Kingdom of the Heavens." 4 "Auspicious are the mourners, for they shall be comforted." 5 "Auspicious are the meek, for they shall inherit the land." 6 "Auspicious are those hungering and thirsting for righteousness, for they shall be satisfied." 7 "Auspicious are the merciful, for they shall be shown mercy." 8 "Auspicious are the pure in heart, for they shall see God." 9 "Auspicious are the peacemakers, for they shall be called sons of God." 10 "Auspicious are those who have been persecuted for the sake of righteousness, for theirs is the Kingdom of the Heavens." 11 "Auspicious are you whenever they might reproach you and persecute and speak all kinds of evil against you on account of me." 12 "Rejoice and be glad, for your reward is great in the heavens; for thus they persecuted the prophets who were before you."

13 Ὑμεῖς ἐστε τὸ ἅλας τῆς γῆς· ἐὰν δὲ τὸ ἅλας μωρανθῇ, ἐν τίνι ἁλισθήσεται; εἰς οὐδὲν ἰσχύει ἔτι εἰ μὴ βληθὲν ἔξω καταπατεῖσθαι ὑπὸ τῶν ἀνθρώπων. 14 Ὑμεῖς ἐστε τὸ φῶς τοῦ κόσμου. οὐ δύναται πόλις κρυβῆναι ἐπάνω ὄρους κειμένη· 15 οὐδὲ καίουσιν λύχνον καὶ τιθέασιν αὐτὸν ὑπὸ τὸν μόδιον ἀλλ' ἐπὶ τὴν λυχνίαν, καὶ λάμπει πᾶσιν τοῖς ἐν τῇ οἰκίᾳ. 16 οὕτως λαμψάτω τὸ φῶς ὑμῶν ἔμπροσθεν τῶν ἀνθρώπων, ὅπως ἴδωσιν ὑμῶν τὰ καλὰ ἔργα καὶ δοξάσωσιν τὸν πατέρα ὑμῶν τὸν ἐν τοῖς οὐρανοῖς. 17 Μὴ νομίσητε ὅτι ἦλθον καταλῦσαι τὸν νόμον ἢ τοὺς προφήτας· οὐκ ἦλθον καταλῦσαι ἀλλὰ πληρῶσαι· 18 ἀμὴν γὰρ λέγω ὑμῖν, ἕως ἂν παρέλθῃ ὁ οὐρανὸς καὶ ἡ γῆ, ἰῶτα ἓν ἢ μία κεραία οὐ μὴ παρέλθῃ ἀπὸ τοῦ νόμου, ἕως ἂν πάντα γένηται. 19 ὃς ἐὰν οὖν λύσῃ μίαν τῶν ἐντολῶν τούτων τῶν ἐλαχίστων καὶ διδάξῃ οὕτως τοὺς ἀνθρώπους, ἐλάχιστος κληθήσεται ἐν τῇ βασιλείᾳ τῶν οὐρανῶν· ὃς δ' ἂν ποιήσῃ καὶ διδάξῃ, οὗτος μέγας κληθήσεται ἐν τῇ βασιλείᾳ τῶν οὐρανῶν. 20 λέγω γὰρ ὑμῖν ὅτι ἐὰν μὴ περισσεύσῃ ὑμῶν ἡ δικαιοσύνη πλεῖον τῶν γραμματέων καὶ Φαρισαίων, οὐ μὴ εἰσέλθητε εἰς τὴν βασιλείαν τῶν οὐρανῶν. 21 Ἠκούσατε ὅτι ἐρρέθη τοῖς ἀρχαίοις· Οὐ φονεύσεις· ὃς δ' ἂν φονεύσῃ, ἔνοχος ἔσται τῇ κρίσει 22 ἐγὼ δὲ λέγω ὑμῖν ὅτι πᾶς ὁ ὀργιζόμενος τῷ ἀδελφῷ αὐτοῦ ἔνοχος ἔσται τῇ κρίσει· ὃς δ' ἂν εἴπῃ τῷ ἀδελφῷ αὐτοῦ· Ῥακά, ἔνοχος ἔσται τῷ συνεδρίῳ· ὃς δ' ἂν εἴπῃ· Μωρέ, ἔνοχος ἔσται εἰς τὴν γέενναν τοῦ πυρός. 23 ἐὰν οὖν προσφέρῃς τὸ δῶρόν σου ἐπὶ τὸ θυσιαστήριον κἀκεῖ μνησθῇς ὅτι ὁ ἀδελφός σου ἔχει τι κατὰ σοῦ, 24 ἄφες ἐκεῖ τὸ δῶρόν σου ἔμπροσθεν τοῦ θυσιαστηρίου καὶ ὕπαγε πρῶτον διαλλάγηθι τῷ ἀδελφῷ σου, καὶ τότε ἐλθὼν πρόσφερε τὸ δῶρόν σου. 25 ἴσθι εὐνοῶν τῷ ἀντιδίκῳ σου ταχὺ ἕως ὅτου εἶ μετ' αὐτοῦ ἐν τῇ ὁδῷ, μήποτέ σε παραδῷ ὁ ἀντίδικος τῷ κριτῇ, καὶ ὁ κριτὴς τῷ ὑπηρέτῃ, καὶ εἰς φυλακὴν βληθήσῃ· 26 ἀμὴν λέγω σοι, οὐ μὴ ἐξέλθῃς ἐκεῖθεν ἕως ἂν ἀποδῷς τὸν ἔσχατον κοδράντην. 27 Ἠκούσατε ὅτι ἐρρέθη· Οὐ μοιχεύσεις. 28 ἐγὼ δὲ λέγω ὑμῖν ὅτι πᾶς ὁ βλέπων γυναῖκα πρὸς τὸ ἐπιθυμῆσαι αὐτὴν ἤδη ἐμοίχευσεν αὐτὴν ἐν τῇ καρδίᾳ αὐτοῦ. 29 εἰ δὲ ὁ ὀφθαλμός σου ὁ δεξιὸς σκανδαλίζει σε, ἔξελε αὐτὸν καὶ βάλε ἀπὸ σοῦ, συμφέρει γάρ σοι ἵνα ἀπόληται ἓν τῶν μελῶν σου καὶ μὴ ὅλον τὸ σῶμά σου βληθῇ εἰς γέενναν. 30 καὶ εἰ ἡ δεξιά σου χεὶρ σκανδαλίζει σε, ἔκκοψον αὐτὴν καὶ βάλε ἀπὸ σοῦ, συμφέρει γάρ σοι ἵνα ἀπόληται ἓν τῶν μελῶν σου καὶ μὴ ὅλον τὸ σῶμά σου εἰς γέενναν ἀπέλθῃ. 31 Ἐρρέθη δέ· Ὃς ἂν ἀπολύσῃ τὴν γυναῖκα αὐτοῦ, δότω αὐτῇ ἀποστάσιον. 32 ἐγὼ δὲ λέγω ὑμῖν ὅτι πᾶς ὁ ἀπολύων τὴν γυναῖκα αὐτοῦ παρεκτὸς λόγου πορνείας ποιεῖ αὐτὴν μοιχευθῆναι, καὶ ὃς ἐὰν ἀπολελυμένην γαμήσῃ μοιχᾶται.

13 "You yourselves are the salt of the earth; but if the salt became tasteless, with what shall it be made salty? It is no longer good for anything except after being cast out to be trampled upon by people. 14 You are the light of the world. A city placed on a hill is not able to be hidden; 15 nor do they light a lamp and put it under the peck-measure but [rather] on the lamp stand, and it shines on everyone in the house. 16 In the same way shine your light before people, so that they may see your good deeds and glorify your Father in the heavens. 17 Do not think that I came to destroy the Law or the Prophets; I came not to destroy but to fulfill; 18 Amen! For I am saying to you, until heaven and earth pass away, one iota or one stroke shall certainly not pass away from the Law, until everything comes to be. 19 Now whoever might destroy one of the least of these commandments and teach people accordingly, he shall be called least in the Kingdom of the Heavens; but whoever should do and teach [them], he shall be called great in the Kingdom of the Heavens. 20 For I am saying to you that unless your righteousness far surpasses that of the Scribes and Pharisees, certainly you shall not enter into the Kingdom of the Heavens. 21 You heard that it was said to the ancients: 'You shall not murder;' so whoever should murder shall be liable to judgment. 22 Moreover, I myself am saying to you that everyone who is angry with his brother shall be liable to judgment; and whoever says to his brother; 'Raca,' shall be liable to the Sanhedrin; and whoever says 'You fool!' shall be liable to the Gehenna of fire. 23 If then, you bring your gift to the altar and there remember that your brother has something against you, 24 leave there your gift in front of the altar and go first to be reconciled to your brother, and then go to bring your gift. 25 Be quickly well-disposed to your opponent while you are on the road with him, so that your opponent may not hand you over to a judge, and the judge to the officer, and you be thrown into prison. 26 Amen! I am saying to you, certainly you will not come out from there until you pay the last Quadrans. 27 You heard that it was said: 'You shall not commit adultery.' 28 Moreover, I myself am saying to you that everyone who is looking at a woman to desire her already committed adultery with her in his heart. 29 So, if your right eye makes you stumble, tear it out and cast it away from you, for it is better for you that one of your members perish and not your whole body be cast into Gehenna. 30 And if your right hand makes you stumble, cut if off and cast it away from you, for it is better for you that one of your members perish and not your whole body go to Gehenna. 31 Now it was said: 'Whoever divorces his wife must give her a certificate of divorce.' 32 Moreover, I am saying to you this: 'Everyone who is divorcing his wife except for a cause of sexual immorality makes her commit adultery, and whoever marries a divorced woman commits adultery.'"

33 Πάλιν ἠκούσατε ὅτι ἐρρέθη τοῖς ἀρχαίοις· Οὐκ ἐπιορκήσεις, ἀποδώσεις δὲ τῷ κυρίῳ τοὺς ὅρκους σου. 34 ἐγὼ δὲ λέγω ὑμῖν μὴ ὀμόσαι ὅλως· μήτε ἐν τῷ οὐρανῷ, ὅτι θρόνος ἐστὶν τοῦ θεοῦ· 35 μήτε ἐν τῇ γῇ, ὅτι ὑποπόδιόν ἐστιν τῶν ποδῶν αὐτοῦ· μήτε εἰς Ἱεροσόλυμα, ὅτι πόλις ἐστὶν τοῦ μεγάλου βασιλέως· 36 μήτε ἐν τῇ κεφαλῇ σου ὀμόσῃς, ὅτι οὐ δύνασαι μίαν τρίχα λευκὴν ποιῆσαι ἢ μέλαιναν. 37 ἔστω δὲ ὁ λόγος ὑμῶν ναὶ ναί, οὒ οὔ· τὸ δὲ περισσὸν τούτων ἐκ τοῦ πονηροῦ ἐστιν. 38 Ἠκούσατε ὅτι ἐρρέθη· Ὀφθαλμὸν ἀντὶ ὀφθαλμοῦ καὶ ὀδόντα ἀντὶ ὀδόντος. 39 ἐγὼ δὲ λέγω ὑμῖν μὴ ἀντιστῆναι τῷ πονηρῷ· ἀλλ' ὅστις σε ῥαπίζει εἰς τὴν δεξιὰν σιαγόνα, στρέψον αὐτῷ καὶ τὴν ἄλλην· 40 καὶ τῷ θέλοντί σοι κριθῆναι καὶ τὸν χιτῶνά σου λαβεῖν, ἄφες αὐτῷ καὶ τὸ ἱμάτιον· 41 καὶ ὅστις σε ἀγγαρεύσει μίλιον ἕν, ὕπαγε μετ' αὐτοῦ δύο. 42 τῷ αἰτοῦντί σε δός, καὶ τὸν θέλοντα ἀπὸ σοῦ δανίσασθαι μὴ ἀποστραφῇς. 43 Ἠκούσατε ὅτι ἐρρέθη· Ἀγαπήσεις τὸν πλησίον σου καὶ μισήσεις τὸν ἐχθρόν σου. 44 ἐγὼ δὲ λέγω ὑμῖν, ἀγαπᾶτε τοὺς ἐχθροὺς ὑμῶν καὶ προσεύχεσθε ὑπὲρ τῶν διωκόντων ὑμᾶς· 45 ὅπως γένησθε υἱοὶ τοῦ πατρὸς ὑμῶν τοῦ ἐν οὐρανοῖς, ὅτι τὸν ἥλιον αὐτοῦ ἀνατέλει ἐπὶ πονηροὺς καὶ ἀγαθοὺς καὶ βρέχει ἐπὶ δικαίους καὶ ἀδίκους. 46 ἐὰν γὰρ ἀγαπήσητε τοὺς ἀγαπῶντας ὑμᾶς, τίνα μισθὸν ἔχετε; οὐχὶ καὶ οἱ τελῶναι τὸ αὐτὸ ποιοῦσιν; 47 καὶ ἐὰν ἀσπάσησθε τοὺς ἀδελφοὺς ὑμῶν μόνον, τί περισσὸν ποιεῖτε; οὐχὶ καὶ οἱ ἐθνικοὶ τὸ αὐτὸ ποιοῦσιν; 48 Ἔσεσθε οὖν ὑμεῖς τέλειοι ὡς ὁ πατὴρ ὑμῶν ὁ οὐράνιος τέλειός ἐστιν.

Κεφ. Ϛ´

6:1 Προσέχετε δὲ τὴν δικαιοσύνην ὑμῶν μὴ ποιεῖν ἔμπροσθεν τῶν ἀνθρώπων πρὸς τὸ θεαθῆναι αὐτοῖς· εἰ δὲ μή γε, μισθὸν οὐκ ἔχετε παρὰ τῷ πατρὶ ὑμῶν τῷ ἐν τοῖς οὐρανοῖς. 2 Ὅταν οὖν ποιῇς ἐλεημοσύνην, μὴ σαλπίσῃς ἔμπροσθέν σου, ὥσπερ οἱ ὑποκριταὶ ποιοῦσιν ἐν ταῖς συναγωγαῖς καὶ ἐν ταῖς ῥύμαις ὅπως δοξασθῶσιν ὑπὸ τῶν ἀνθρώπων· ἀμὴν λέγω ὑμῖν ἀπέχουσιν τὸν μισθὸν αὐτῶν. 3 σοῦ δὲ ποιοῦντος ἐλεημοσύνην μὴ γνώτω ἡ ἀριστερά σου τί ποιεῖ ἡ δεξιά σου, 4 ὅπως ᾖ σου ἡ ἐλεημοσύνη ἐν τῷ κρυπτῷ· καὶ ὁ πατήρ σου ὁ βλέπων ἐν τῷ κρυπτῷ ἀποδώσει σοι. 5 Καὶ ὅταν προσεύχησθε, οὐκ ἔσεσθε ὡς οἱ ὑποκριταί· ὅτι φιλοῦσιν ἐν ταῖς συναγωγαῖς καὶ ἐν ταῖς γωνίαις τῶν πλατειῶν ἑστῶτες προσεύχεσθαι, ὅπως φανῶσιν τοῖς ἀνθρώποις· ἀμὴν λέγω ὑμῖν, ἀπέχουσι τὸν μισθὸν αὐτῶν. 6 σὺ δὲ ὅταν προσεύχῃ, εἴσελθε εἰς τὸ ταμεῖόν σου καὶ κλείσας τὴν θύραν σου πρόσευξαι τῷ πατρί σου τῷ ἐν τῷ κρυπτῷ· καὶ ὁ πατήρ σου ὁ βλέπων ἐν τῷ κρυπτῷ ἀποδώσει σοι. 7 Προσευχόμενοι δὲ μὴ βατταλογήσητε ὥσπερ οἱ ἐθνικοί, δοκοῦσιν γὰρ ὅτι ἐν τῇ πολυλογίᾳ αὐτῶν εἰσακουσθήσονται· 8 μὴ οὖν ὁμοιωθῆτε αὐτοῖς, οἶδεν γὰρ ὁ πατὴρ ὑμῶν ὧν χρείαν ἔχετε πρὸ τοῦ ὑμᾶς αἰτῆσαι αὐτόν.

33 "Again, you heard that is was said to the ancients, 'You shall not swear falsely, but you shall fulfill your oaths to the Lord.' 34 But I myself am telling you not to swear at all; neither by heaven, because it is the throne of God; 35 nor by earth, because it is a footstool for His feet; nor by Jerusalem, because it is the city of the great king; 36 nor should you swear by your head, because you are not able to make one hair white or black. 37 But let your word yes [be] yes, no [be] no; now that which exceeds these things is from the evil one. 38 You heard that it was said, 'An eye for an eye and a tooth for a tooth.' 39 But I myself am telling you not to resist an evildoer; but whoever slaps you on the right cheek, turn also the other toward him; 40 and the one wishing to take you to court and take your tunic, give to him your clothing also; 41 and whoever forces you [to go] one mile, go with him for two. 42 Give to the one asking you, and do not turn away from the one wishing to borrow from you. 43 You heard that it was said, 'You shall love your neighbor and hate your enemy.' 44 But I myself am saying to you, 'Love your enemies and pray for those who persecute you;' 45 in this way you become sons of your Father who is in the heavens, because he makes his sun rise upon the evil and good and sends rain upon the righteous and unrighteous. 46 For if you love those who love you, what reward do you have? Do the tax collectors not also do this? 47 And if you only greet your brothers, what remarkable thing do you do? Do the Gentiles not also do this? 48 You therefore shall be mature like your Father who is in heaven is mature. 6:1 So be careful not to practice your righteousness before people to be seen by them; otherwise you do not have a reward with your Father in the heavens. 2 So when you give alms, do not sound a trumpet before you, just as the hypocrites do in the synagogues and the streets, so that they may be honored by people; Amen! I am saying to you, 'They have their reward.' 3 But you, while giving alms, do not let your left hand know what your right hand does, 4 so that your almsgiving may be in secret; and your Father who sees in secret shall repay you. 5 And when you pray, you shall not be as the hypocrites; for they love, in the synagogues, and in the street corners, to pray standing, so that they may be seen by people; Amen! I am saying to you, 'They have their reward.' 6 But when you yourselves pray, enter into your inner room and after shutting your door pray to your Father who is in secret; and your Father who sees in secret shall repay you. 7 So when you are praying do not use meaningless repetition just as the Gentiles, for they think that with their many words they shall be heard; 8 then do not be like them, for your Father knows what you need before you ask him."

Matthew 6:9-24

9 Οὕτως οὖν προσεύχεσθε ὑμεῖς· Πάτερ ἡμῶν ὁ ἐν τοῖς οὐρανοῖς· ἁγιασθήτω τὸ ὄνομά σου, 10 ἐλθέτω ἡ βασιλεία σου, γενηθήτω τὸ θέλημά σου, ὡς ἐν οὐρανῷ καὶ ἐπὶ γῆς· 11 τὸν ἄρτον ἡμῶν τὸν ἐπιούσιον δὸς ἡμῖν σήμερον· 12 καὶ ἄφες ἡμῖν τὰ ὀφειλήματα ἡμῶν, ὡς καὶ ἡμεῖς ἀφήκαμεν τοῖς ὀφειλέταις ἡμῶν·

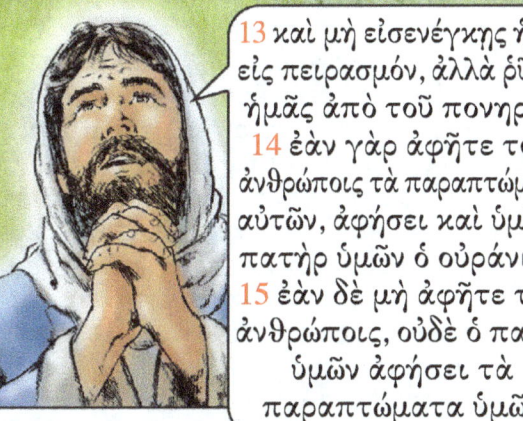

13 καὶ μὴ εἰσενέγκῃς ἡμᾶς εἰς πειρασμόν, ἀλλὰ ῥῦσαι ἡμᾶς ἀπὸ τοῦ πονηροῦ. 14 ἐὰν γὰρ ἀφῆτε τοῖς ἀνθρώποις τὰ παραπτώματα αὐτῶν, ἀφήσει καὶ ὑμῖν ὁ πατὴρ ὑμῶν ὁ οὐράνιος· 15 ἐὰν δὲ μὴ ἀφῆτε τοῖς ἀνθρώποις, οὐδὲ ὁ πατὴρ ὑμῶν ἀφήσει τὰ παραπτώματα ὑμῶν.

16 Ὅταν δὲ νηστεύητε, μὴ γίνεσθε ὡς οἱ ὑποκριταὶ σκυθρωποί, ἀφανίζουσιν γὰρ τὰ πρόσωπα αὐτῶν ὅπως φανῶσιν τοῖς ἀνθρώποις νηστεύοντες· ἀμὴν λέγω ὑμῖν, ἀπέχουσιν τὸν μισθὸν αὐτῶν. 17 σὺ δὲ νηστεύων ἄλειψαί σου τὴν κεφαλὴν καὶ τὸ πρόσωπόν σου νίψαι, 18 ὅπως μὴ φανῇς τοῖς ἀνθρώποις νηστεύων ἀλλὰ τῷ πατρί σου τῷ ἐν τῷ κρυφαίῳ· καὶ ὁ πατήρ σου ὁ βλέπων ἐν τῷ κρυφαίῳ ἀποδώσει σοι. 19 Μὴ θησαυρίζετε ὑμῖν θησαυροὺς ἐπὶ τῆς γῆς, ὅπου σὴς καὶ βρῶσις ἀφανίζει, καὶ ὅπου κλέπται διορύσσουσιν καὶ κλέπτουσιν· 20 θησαυρίζετε δὲ ὑμῖν θησαυροὺς ἐν οὐρανῷ, ὅπου οὔτε σὴς οὔτε βρῶσις ἀφανίζει, καὶ ὅπου κλέπται οὐ δι ορύσσουσιν οὐδὲ κλέπτουσιν· 21 ὅπου γάρ ἐστιν ὁ θησαυρός σου, ἐκεῖ ἔσται καὶ ἡ καρδία σου. 22 Ὁ λύχνος τοῦ σώματός ἐστιν ὁ ὀφθαλμός. ἐὰν οὖν ᾖ ὁ ὀφθαλμός σου ἁπλοῦς, ὅλον τὸ σῶμά σου φωτεινὸν ἔσται· 23 ἐὰν δὲ ὁ ὀφθαλμός σου πονηρὸς ᾖ, ὅλον τὸ σῶμά σου σκοτεινὸν ἔσται. εἰ οὖν τὸ φῶς τὸ ἐν σοὶ σκότος ἐστίν, τὸ σκότος πόσον. 24 Οὐδεὶς δύναται δυσὶ κυρίοις δουλεύειν· ἢ γὰρ τὸν ἕνα μισήσει καὶ τὸν ἕτερον ἀγαπήσει, ἢ ἑνὸς ἀνθέξεται καὶ τοῦ ἑτέρου καταφρονήσει. οὐ δύνασθε θεῷ δουλεύειν καὶ μαμωνᾷ.

9 "So then you yourselves pray in this manner, 'Our Father who [is] in the heavens; let your name be hallowed, 10 let your kingdom come, let your will be done, as in heaven also on earth; 11 our daily bread give us today; 12 and forgive us our debts, as we also forgive our debtors; 13 and lead us not into temptation, but deliver us from the evil one.' 14 For if you forgive people their trespasses, your heavenly Father will also forgive you; 15 but if you do not forgive people, nor will your Father forgive your trespasses. 16 Now when you fast, do not be like the hypocrites, gloomy, for they make their faces unrecognizable in order to appear to people to be fasting; Amen! I am saying to you, they have their reward in full. 17 But you, when fasting, anoint your head and wash your face, 18 in order that you may not appear to be fasting to people except to your Father who is in secret; and your Father who sees in secret shall repay you. 19 Do not store up for yourselves treasure on the earth, where moth and rust destroy, and where thieves break in and steal; 20 but store up for yourselves treasure in heaven, where neither moth nor rust destroy, and where thieves do not break in nor steal; 21 for where your treasure is, there shall be your heart also. 22 The lamp of the body is the eye. If then your eye is sincere, your whole body shall be full of light; 23 but if your eye is evil, your whole body shall be full of darkness. If then the light which is in you is darkness, how great [is] the darkness! 24 No one is able to serve two Lords; for either he shall hate the one and love the other, or he shall hold on to one and despise the other. You are not able to serve God and Mammon."

Matthew 6:25-7:14

25 Διὰ τοῦτο λέγω ὑμῖν· μὴ μεριμνᾶτε τῇ ψυχῇ ὑμῶν τί φάγητε, μηδὲ τῷ σώματι ὑμῶν τί ἐνδύσησθε· οὐχὶ ἡ ψυχὴ πλεῖόν ἐστι τῆς τροφῆς καὶ τὸ σῶμα τοῦ ἐνδύματος; 26 ἐμβλέψατε εἰς τὰ πετεινὰ τοῦ οὐρανοῦ ὅτι οὐ σπείρουσιν οὐδὲ θερίζουσιν οὐδὲ συνάγουσιν εἰς ἀποθήκας, καὶ ὁ πατὴρ ὑμῶν ὁ οὐράνιος τρέφει αὐτά· οὐχ ὑμεῖς μᾶλλον διαφέρετε αὐτῶν; 27 τίς δὲ ἐξ ὑμῶν μεριμνῶν δύναται προσθεῖναι ἐπὶ τὴν ἡλικίαν αὐτοῦ πῆχυν ἕνα; 28 καὶ περὶ ἐνδύματος τί μεριμνᾶτε; καταμάθετε τὰ κρίνα τοῦ ἀγροῦ πῶς αὐξάνουσιν· οὐ κοπιῶσιν οὐδὲ νήθουσιν· 29 λέγω δὲ ὑμῖν ὅτι οὐδὲ Σολομὼν ἐν πάσῃ τῇ δόξῃ αὐτοῦ περιεβάλετο ὡς ἓν τούτων. 30 εἰ δὲ τὸν χόρτον τοῦ ἀγροῦ σήμερον ὄντα καὶ αὔριον εἰς κλίβανον βαλλόμενον ὁ θεὸς οὕτως ἀμφιέννυσιν, οὐ πολλῷ μᾶλλον ὑμᾶς, ὀλιγόπιστοι; 31 μὴ οὖν μεριμνήσητε λέγοντες· Τί φάγωμεν; ἤ· Τί πίωμεν; ἤ· Τί περιβαλώμεθα; 32 πάντα γὰρ ταῦτα τὰ ἔθνη ἐπιζητοῦσιν· οἶδεν γὰρ ὁ πατὴρ ὑμῶν ὁ οὐράνιος ὅτι χρῄζετε τούτων ἁπάντων. 33 ζητεῖτε δὲ πρῶτον τὴν βασιλείαν καὶ τὴν δικαιοσύνην αὐτοῦ, καὶ ταῦτα πάντα προστεθήσεται ὑμῖν. 34 μὴ οὖν μεριμνήσητε εἰς τὴν αὔριον, ἡ γὰρ αὔριον μεριμνήσει αὑτῆς· ἀρκετὸν τῇ ἡμέρᾳ ἡ κακία αὐτῆς.

Κεφ. Ζʹ

7:1 Μὴ κρίνετε, ἵνα μὴ κριθῆτε· 2 ἐν ᾧ γὰρ κρίματι κρίνετε κριθήσεσθε, καὶ ἐν ᾧ μέτρῳ μετρεῖτε μετρηθήσεται ὑμῖν. 3 τί δὲ βλέπεις τὸ κάρφος τὸ ἐν τῷ ὀφθαλμῷ τοῦ ἀδελφοῦ σου, τὴν δὲ ἐν τῷ σῷ ὀφθαλμῷ δοκὸν οὐ κατανοεῖς; 4 ἢ πῶς ἐρεῖς τῷ ἀδελφῷ σου· Ἄφες ἐκβάλω τὸ κάρφος ἐκ τοῦ ὀφθαλμοῦ σου, καὶ ἰδοὺ ἡ δοκὸς ἐν τῷ ὀφθαλμῷ σοῦ; 5 ὑποκριτά, ἔκβαλε πρῶτον ἐκ τοῦ ὀφθαλμοῦ σοῦ τὴν δοκόν, καὶ τότε διαβλέψεις ἐκβαλεῖν τὸ κάρφος ἐκ τοῦ ὀφθαλμοῦ τοῦ ἀδελφοῦ σου. 6 Μὴ δῶτε τὸ ἅγιον τοῖς κυσίν, μηδὲ βάλητε τοὺς μαργαρίτας ὑμῶν ἔμπροσθεν τῶν χοίρων, μήποτε καταπατήσουσιν αὐτοὺς ἐν τοῖς ποσὶν αὐτῶν καὶ στραφέντες ῥήξωσιν ὑμᾶς. 7 Αἰτεῖτε, καὶ δοθήσεται ὑμῖν· ζητεῖτε, καὶ εὑρήσετε· κρούετε, καὶ ἀνοιγήσεται ὑμῖν. 8 πᾶς γὰρ ὁ αἰτῶν λαμβάνει καὶ ὁ ζητῶν εὑρίσκει καὶ τῷ κρούοντι ἀνοιγήσεται. 9 ἢ τίς ἐστιν ἐξ ὑμῶν ἄνθρωπος, ὃν αἰτήσει ὁ υἱὸς αὐτοῦ ἄρτον — μὴ λίθον ἐπιδώσει αὐτῷ; 10 ἢ καὶ ἰχθὺν αἰτήσει — μὴ ὄφιν ἐπιδώσει αὐτῷ; 11 εἰ οὖν ὑμεῖς πονηροὶ ὄντες οἴδατε δόματα ἀγαθὰ διδόναι τοῖς τέκνοις ὑμῶν, πόσῳ μᾶλλον ὁ πατὴρ ὑμῶν ὁ ἐν τοῖς οὐρανοῖς δώσει ἀγαθὰ τοῖς αἰτοῦσιν αὐτόν. 12 Πάντα οὖν ὅσα ἐὰν θέλητε ἵνα ποιῶσιν ὑμῖν οἱ ἄνθρωποι, οὕτως καὶ ὑμεῖς ποιεῖτε αὐτοῖς· οὗτος γάρ ἐστιν ὁ νόμος καὶ οἱ προφῆται. 13 Εἰσέλθατε διὰ τῆς στενῆς πύλης· ὅτι πλατεῖα ἡ πύλη καὶ εὐρύχωρος ἡ ὁδὸς ἡ ἀπάγουσα εἰς τὴν ἀπώλειαν, καὶ πολλοί εἰσιν οἱ εἰσερχόμενοι δι' αὐτῆς· 14 ὅτι στενὴ ἡ πύλη καὶ τεθλιμμένη ἡ ὁδὸς ἡ ἀπάγουσα εἰς τὴν ζωήν, καὶ ὀλίγοι εἰσὶν οἱ εὑρίσκοντες αὐτήν.

25 "Because of this I am saying to you; do not be anxious about your lives, what to eat, nor your bodies, what to put on; is life not more than food and the body more than clothes? 26 Consider closely the birds of heaven that they do not sow nor reap nor gather into storehouses, and your Father who is in heaven nourishes them; 27 now [are] you not worth more than them? So who of you, being anxious, is able to add unto his life one cubit? 28 And concerning clothes, why are you anxious? Observe the lilies of the field how they grow; they do not toil nor spin; 29 now I am saying to you that not even Solomon in all his glory dressed as one of these. 30 But if God dresses the grass of the field like this today and tomorrow is throwing it into a furnace, how much more so [will he clothe] you, you of little faith? 31 Then do not be anxious saying, 'What shall we eat?' or, 'What shall we drink?' or, 'What shall we wear?' 32 For all these things the Gentiles seek; for your Father who is in heaven knows that you need all these things. 33 But seek first the kingdom and His righteousness, and all these things shall be added to you. 34 Then do not worry about tomorrow, for tomorrow shall worry about itself; sufficient for the day [is] its own evil. 7:1 Do not judge, so that you may not be judged. 2 For with which judgment you judge you shall be judged, and with which measure you measure you yourselves shall be measured. 3 Now why do you see the speck in the eye of your brother, but do not consider the log in your eye? 4 Or how do you say to your brother, 'Allow me to cast out the speck from your eye,' and behold, the log [is] in your eye? 5 Hypocrite! First cast away from your eye the log, and then you shall see clearly to cast out the speck from the eye of your brother. 6 Do not give what is holy to the dogs, nor throw your pearls before the swine, lest they shall trample them under their feet and turning around might tear you to pieces. 7 Ask, and [it] shall be given to you; seek, and you shall find; knock, and [it] shall be opened to you. 8 For everyone who is asking receives and the one who is seeking finds and the one who is knocking [it] shall be opened. 9 Or which person is there among you, who [when] his son shall ask for bread – shall give him a stone? [No one!] 10 Or even [when] he shall ask for a fish shall give him a serpent? [None!] 11 If then you, being evil, know to give good gifts to your children, how much more shall your Father who is in the heavens give good things to those asking Him. 12 Then everything that you wish that people should do to you, thus also you do to them; for this is the Law and the Prophets. 13 Enter through the narrow gate; for broad [is] the gate and wide [is] the road which is leading to destruction, and many are those entering through it; 14 for narrow [is] the gate and confined [is] the road which is leading to life, and few are those who find it."

Matthew 7:15-8:2

15 Προσέχετε ἀπὸ τῶν ψευδοπροφητῶν, οἵτινες ἔρχονται πρὸς ὑμᾶς ἐν ἐνδύμασι προβάτων ἔσωθεν δέ εἰσιν λύκοι ἅρπαγες. **16** ἀπὸ τῶν καρπῶν αὐτῶν ἐπιγνώσεσθε αὐτούς. μήτι συλλέγουσιν ἀπὸ ἀκανθῶν σταφυλὰς ἢ ἀπὸ τριβόλων σῦκα; **17** οὕτως πᾶν δένδρον ἀγαθὸν καρποὺς καλοὺς ποιεῖ, τὸ δὲ σαπρὸν δένδρον καρποὺς πονηροὺς ποιεῖ· **18** οὐ δύναται δένδρον ἀγαθὸν καρποὺς πονηροὺς ποιεῖν, οὐδὲ δένδρον σαπρὸν καρποὺς καλοὺς ποιεῖν. **19** πᾶν δένδρον μὴ ποιοῦν καρπὸν καλὸν ἐκκόπτεται καὶ εἰς πῦρ βάλλεται. **20** ἄρα γε ἀπὸ τῶν καρπῶν αὐτῶν ἐπιγνώσεσθε αὐτούς. **21** Οὐ πᾶς ὁ λέγων μοι· Κύριε κύριε εἰσελεύσεται εἰς τὴν βασιλείαν τῶν οὐρανῶν, ἀλλ' ὁ ποιῶν τὸ θέλημα τοῦ πατρός μου τοῦ ἐν τοῖς οὐρανοῖς. **22** πολλοὶ ἐροῦσίν μοι ἐν ἐκείνῃ τῇ ἡμέρᾳ· Κύριε κύριε, οὐ τῷ σῷ ὀνόματι ἐπροφητεύσαμεν, καὶ τῷ σῷ ὀνόματι δαιμόνια ἐξεβάλομεν, καὶ τῷ σῷ ὀνόματι δυνάμεις πολλὰς ἐποιήσαμεν; **23** καὶ τότε ὁμολογήσω αὐτοῖς ὅτι Οὐδέποτε ἔγνων ὑμᾶς· ἀποχωρεῖτε ἀπ' ἐμοῦ οἱ ἐργαζόμενοι τὴν ἀνομίαν. **24** Πᾶς οὖν ὅστις ἀκούει μου τοὺς λόγους τούτους καὶ ποιεῖ αὐτούς, ὁμοιωθήσεται ἀνδρὶ φρονίμῳ, ὅστις ᾠκοδόμησεν αὐτοῦ τὴν οἰκίαν ἐπὶ τὴν πέτραν. **25** καὶ κατέβη ἡ βροχὴ καὶ ἦλθον οἱ ποταμοὶ καὶ ἔπνευσαν οἱ ἄνεμοι καὶ προσέπεσαν τῇ οἰκίᾳ ἐκείνῃ, καὶ οὐκ ἔπεσεν, τεθεμελίωτο γὰρ ἐπὶ τὴν πέτραν. **26** καὶ πᾶς ὁ ἀκούων μου τοὺς λόγους τούτους καὶ μὴ ποιῶν αὐτοὺς ὁμοιωθήσεται ἀνδρὶ μωρῷ, ὅστις ᾠκοδόμησεν αὐτοῦ τὴν οἰκίαν ἐπὶ τὴν ἄμμον. **27** καὶ κατέβη ἡ βροχὴ καὶ ἦλθον οἱ ποταμοὶ καὶ ἔπνευσαν οἱ ἄνεμοι καὶ προσέκοψαν τῇ οἰκίᾳ ἐκείνῃ, καὶ ἔπεσεν, καὶ ἦν ἡ πτῶσις αὐτῆς μεγάλη.

28 Καὶ ἐγένετο ὅτε ἐτέλεσεν ὁ Ἰησοῦς τοὺς λόγους τούτους, ἐξεπλήσσοντο οἱ ὄχλοι ἐπὶ τῇ διδαχῇ αὐτοῦ· **29** ἦν γὰρ διδάσκων αὐτοὺς ὡς ἐξουσίαν ἔχων καὶ οὐχ ὡς οἱ γραμματεῖς αὐτῶν.

Κεφ. Η΄

8:1 Καταβάντος δὲ αὐτοῦ ἀπὸ τοῦ ὄρους ἠκολούθησαν αὐτῷ ὄχλοι πολλοί.

2 καὶ ἰδοὺ λεπρὸς προσελθὼν προσεκύνει αὐτῷ λέγων·

Κύριε, ἐὰν θέλῃς δύνασαί με καθαρίσαι.

15 "Watch out for the false prophets, who come to you in sheep's clothing but inside they are ravenous wolves. **16** From their fruits you shall know them. Do [people] collect grapes from thorn bushes or figs from thistles? [No!]. **17** In the same way every good tree produces good fruits, but the rotten tree produces evil fruits; **18** a good tree is not able to produce evil fruits, nor a rotten tree to produce good fruits. **19** Every tree which is not producing good fruit is cut off and cast into a fire. **20** Then indeed you shall know them by their fruits. **21** Not all who are saying to me, 'Lord Lord' shall enter into the Kingdom of the Heavens, but the one who is doing the will of my Father who is in the heavens. **22** Many shall say to me on that day, 'Lord Lord, did we not prophesy in your name, and in your name cast out demons, and in your name do many mighty things?' **23** And then I shall profess to them this: 'I never knew you; away from me you who practice lawlessness.' **24** Then everyone who hears these words of mine and does them, is like a wise man, who built his house on the rock. **25** And the rain descended and the rivers came and the winds blew and beat against that house, and it did not fall, for it had been founded on the rock. **26** And everyone who is hearing these words of mine and is not doing them he shall be like a foolish man, who built his house on the sand. **27** And the rain descended and the rivers came and the winds blew and beat against that house, and it fell, and its fall was great." **28** And it happened when Jesus finished these words, the crowds were marveling at his teaching; **29** for he was teaching them as one having power and not as their scribes. **8:1** Now having descended from the mountain great crowds followed him. **2** And behold a man with a skin disease, approaching, was bowing down before him saying, "Lord, if you are willing you can cleanse me."

Matthew 8:3-9

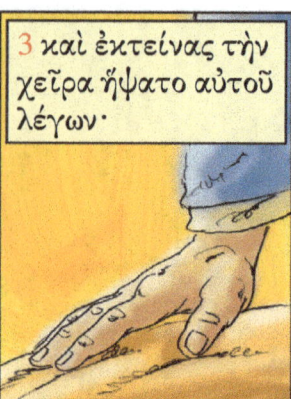
3 καὶ ἐκτείνας τὴν χεῖρα ἥψατο αὐτοῦ λέγων·

Θέλω, καθαρίσθητι·

καὶ εὐθέως ἐκαθαρίσθη αὐτοῦ ἡ λέπρα.

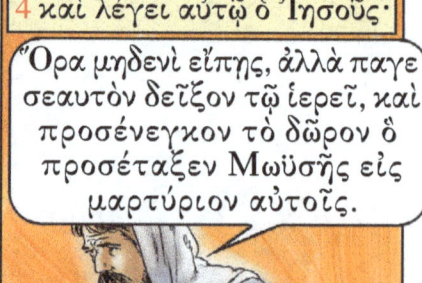
4 καὶ λέγει αὐτῷ ὁ Ἰησοῦς· "Ὅρα μηδενὶ εἴπῃς, ἀλλὰ ὕπαγε σεαυτὸν δεῖξον τῷ ἱερεῖ, καὶ προσένεγκον τὸ δῶρον ὃ προσέταξεν Μωϋσῆς εἰς μαρτύριον αὐτοῖς.

5 Εἰσελθόντος δὲ αὐτοῦ εἰς Καφαρναοὺμ προσῆλθεν αὐτῷ ἑκατόνταρχος παρακαλῶν αὐτὸν 6 καὶ λέγων·

Κύριε, ὁ παῖς μου βέβληται ἐν τῇ οἰκίᾳ παραλυτικός, δεινῶς βασανιζόμενος.

7 καὶ λέγει αὐτῷ·

Ἐγὼ ἐλθὼν θεραπεύσω αὐτόν.

8 καὶ ἀποκριθεὶς ὁ ἑκατόνταρχος ἔφη·

Κύριε, οὐκ εἰμὶ ἱκανὸς ἵνα μου ὑπὸ τὴν στέγην εἰσέλθῃς· ἀλλὰ μόνον εἰπὲ λόγῳ, καὶ ἰαθήσεται ὁ παῖς μου· 9 καὶ γὰρ ἐγὼ ἄνθρωπός εἰμι ὑπὸ ἐξουσίαν, ἔχων ὑπ' ἐμαυτὸν στρατιώτας, καὶ λέγω τούτῳ· Πορεύθητι, καὶ πορεύεται, καὶ ἄλλῳ· Ἔρχου, καὶ ἔρχεται, καὶ τῷ δούλῳ μου· Ποίησον τοῦτο, καὶ ποιεῖ.

3 And stretching out the hand he touched him saying, "I am willing, be cleansed;" and immediately his skin disease was cleansed. 4 And Jesus says to him, "See [that] you tell no one, but go! show yourself to the priest! And bring the gift which Moses commanded as a testimony to them." 5 Now after he entered Capernaum a Centurion came to him beseeching him 6 and saying, "Lord, my servant has been laid down in the house paralyzed, terribly tormented." 7 And he says to him, "When I come I shall heal him." 8 And answering back the Centurion said, "Lord, I am not worthy to have you enter under my roof; but only speak a word, and my servant shall be healed. 9 For I am also a man under authority, having under me soldiers, and I say to this one, 'Go', and he goes, and to another, 'Come,' and he comes, and to my servant, 'Do this,' and he does."

Matthew 8:10-16

[10] But when Jesus heard [this] he marveled and said to those following, [11] "Amen! I am saying to you, I have not found anyone in Israel with such faith. Now I am saying to you that many from the east and west shall come and recline with Abraham and Isaac and Jacob in the Kingdom of the Heavens; [12] but the sons of the kingdom shall be cast out into the outer darkness; in that place there shall be weeping and gnashing of teeth." [13] And Jesus said to the Centurion, "Go, as you believed so it will happen to you;" and the servant was healed in that hour. [14] And coming into the house of Peter, Jesus saw that his mother-in-law was laid down and suffered a fever; [15] and he stretched out his hand, and the fever left her, and she was raised up and was serving them. [16] Now when evening came they brought to him many who were demon-possessed; and he cast out the spirits with a word, and all those having ailments he healed;

Matthew 8:17-24

[17] so that which was spoken by Isaiah the prophet would be fulfilled saying, "He took our weaknesses and bore our diseases." [18] But when Jesus saw great crowds around him he gave orders to leave to the other side. [19] And after one scribe came he said to him, "Teacher, I will follow you wherever you go." [20] And Jesus says to him, "The foxes have holes and the birds of the sky a place to nest, but the Son of Man does not have a place to rest the head. [21] Additionally, another of the disciples said to him, "Lord, permit me first to depart and bury my father." [22] But Jesus says to him, "Follow me, and let the dead bury their dead." [23] And when he embarked onto a boat his disciples followed him. [24] And behold, a great storm raged on the sea, so that the boat was being covered by the waves, but he was sleeping.

Matthew 8:25-32

25 And having come toward him, they woke him saying, "Lord, save [us], we are perishing!" 26 And he says to them, "Why are you afraid. You of little faith?" Then having risen he rebuked the waves and the sea, and there was a great silence. 27 Now the men marveled saying, "What kind of man is this that the waves and the sea obey him?" 28 And after coming to the other side to the region of the Gadarenes two demon possessed men met him coming out from the tombs, [being] exceedingly difficult to deal with so that no one was able to pass through by that road. 29 And behold they cried out saying, "What do our [affairs have to do with] yours, Son of God? Have you come here before the time to torment us?" 30 Now far away from them was a great herd of feeding pigs. 31 So the demons were pleading with him saying, "If you cast us out, send us into the herd of pigs." 32 And he said to the them, "Go!" So they came out and went into the pigs; and behold the whole herd rushed down the cliff into the sea, and died in the waters.

Matthew 8:33-9:8

33 οἱ δὲ βόσκοντες ἔφυγον, καὶ ἀπελθόντες εἰς τὴν πόλιν ἀπήγγειλαν πάντα καὶ τὰ τῶν δαιμονιζομένων. 34 καὶ ἰδοὺ πᾶσα ἡ πόλις ἐξῆλθεν εἰς ὑπάντησιν τῷ Ἰησοῦ, καὶ ἰδόντες αὐτὸν παρεκάλεσαν ὅπως μεταβῇ ἀπὸ τῶν ὁρίων αὐτῶν.

Κεφ. Θ´

9:1 Καὶ ἐμβὰς εἰς πλοῖον διεπέρασεν καὶ ἦλθεν εἰς τὴν ἰδίαν πόλιν.

2 Καὶ ἰδοὺ προσέφερον αὐτῷ παραλυτικὸν ἐπὶ κλίνης βεβλημένον.

Καὶ ἰδὼν ὁ Ἰησοῦς τὴν πίστιν αὐτῶν εἶπεν τῷ παραλυτικῷ·

Θάρσει, τέκνον· ἀφίενταί σου αἱ ἁμαρτίαι.

3 καὶ ἰδού τινες τῶν γραμματέων εἶπαν ἐν ἑαυτοῖς·

Οὗτος βλασφημεῖ.

4 καὶ εἰδὼς ὁ Ἰησοῦς τὰς ἐνθυμήσεις αὐτῶν εἶπεν

Ἱνατί ἐνθυμεῖσθε πονηρὰ ἐν ταῖς καρδίαις ὑμῶν; 5 τί γάρ ἐστιν εὐκοπώτερον, εἰπεῖν· Ἀφίενταί σου αἱ ἁμαρτίαι, ἢ εἰπεῖν· Ἔγειρε καὶ περιπάτει; 6 ἵνα δὲ εἰδῆτε ὅτι ἐξουσίαν ἔχει ὁ υἱὸς τοῦ ἀνθρώπου ἐπὶ τῆς γῆς ἀφιέναι ἁμαρτίας — τότε λέγει τῷ παραλυτικῷ·

Ἐγερθεὶς ἆρόν σου τὴν κλίνην καὶ ὕπαγε εἰς τὸν οἶκόν σου.

7 καὶ ἐγερθεὶς ἀπῆλθεν εἰς τὸν οἶκον αὐτοῦ.

8 ἰδόντες δὲ οἱ ὄχλοι ἐφοβήθησαν καὶ ἐδόξασαν τὸν θεὸν τὸν δόντα ἐξουσίαν τοιαύτην τοῖς ἀνθρώποις.

33 Now the herdsmen fled, and after coming into the city they reported everything also [about] the demon possessed. 34 And behold the city came out to meet Jesus, and seeing him they pleaded in order that he might depart from their region. 9:1 And embarking unto the boat he crossed over and came to his own city. 2 And behold they were bringing to him a paralytic placed on a mat. And Jesus seeing their faith said to the paralytic, "Be of good courage child; your sins are forgiven." 3 And behold some of the scribes said among themselves, "This man is blaspheming!" 4 And knowing their thoughts Jesus said, "Why are you contemplating evil in your hearts?" 5 For what is easier, to say, 'Your sins are forgiven,' or to say, 'Arise and walk?' 6 Now so that you may know that the Son of Man has authority to forgive sins on earth" – then he says to the paralytic, "Arise to pick up your mat and go to your house." 7 And after arising he went to his house. 8 But when the crowds saw [this] they were afraid and glorified God who gives such power to humans.

Matthew 9:9-17

9 Καὶ παράγων ὁ Ἰησοῦς ἐκεῖθεν εἶδεν ἄνθρωπον καθήμενον ἐπὶ τὸ τελώνιον, Μαθθαῖον λεγόμενον, καὶ λέγει αὐτῷ·

Ἀκολούθει μοι·

καὶ ἀναστὰς ἠκολούθησεν αὐτῷ.

10 Καὶ ἐγένετο αὐτοῦ ἀνακειμένου ἐν τῇ οἰκίᾳ, καὶ ἰδοὺ πολλοὶ τελῶναι καὶ ἁμαρτωλοὶ ἐλθόντες συνανέκειντο τῷ Ἰησοῦ καὶ τοῖς μαθηταῖς αὐτοῦ.

11 καὶ ἰδόντες οἱ Φαρισαῖοι ἔλεγον τοῖς μαθηταῖς αὐτοῦ·

Διὰ τί μετὰ τῶν τελωνῶν καὶ ἁμαρτωλῶν ἐσθίει ὁ διδάσκαλος ὑμῶν;

12 ὁ δὲ ἀκούσας εἶπεν·

Οὐ χρείαν ἔχουσιν οἱ ἰσχύοντες ἰατροῦ ἀλλὰ οἱ κακῶς ἔχοντες.

13 πορευθέντες δὲ μάθετε τί ἐστιν· Ἔλεος θέλω καὶ οὐ θυσίαν· οὐ γὰρ ἦλθον καλέσαι δικαίους ἀλλὰ ἁμαρτωλούς

14 Τότε προσέρχονται αὐτῷ οἱ μαθηταὶ Ἰωάννου λέγοντες·

Διὰ τί ἡμεῖς καὶ οἱ Φαρισαῖοι νηστεύομεν πολλά, οἱ δὲ μαθηταί σου οὐ νηστεύουσιν;

15 καὶ εἶπεν αὐτοῖς ὁ Ἰησοῦς·

Μὴ δύνανται οἱ υἱοὶ τοῦ νυμφῶνος πενθεῖν ἐφ' ὅσον μετ' αὐτῶν ἐστιν ὁ νυμφίος; ἐλεύσονται δὲ ἡμέραι ὅταν ἀπαρθῇ ἀπ' αὐτῶν ὁ νυμφίος, καὶ τότε νηστεύσουσιν. 16 οὐδεὶς δὲ ἐπιβάλλει ἐπίβλημα ῥάκους ἀγνάφου ἐπὶ ἱματίῳ παλαιῷ· αἴρει γὰρ τὸ πλήρωμα αὐτοῦ ἀπὸ τοῦ ἱματίου, καὶ χεῖρον σχίσμα γίνεται. 17 οὐδὲ βάλλουσιν οἶνον νέον εἰς ἀσκοὺς παλαιούς· εἰ δὲ μή γε, ῥήγνυνται οἱ ἀσκοί, καὶ ὁ οἶνος ἐκχεῖται καὶ οἱ ἀσκοὶ ἀπόλλυνται· ἀλλὰ βάλλουσιν οἶνον νέον εἰς ἀσκοὺς καινούς, καὶ ἀμφότεροι συντηροῦνται.

9 And passing by from that place Jesus saw a man sitting in the tax office, called Matthew, and he says to him, "Follow me;" and after getting up he followed him. 10 And it happened as he was reclining in the house, and behold many tax collectors and sinners, coming, were reclining with Jesus and his disciples. 11 And seeing [this] the Pharisees were saying to his disciples, "Why does your teacher eat with the tax collectors and sinners?" 12 But when he heard [this] he said, "The healthy do not have a need for a physician but the sick do. 13 Now, go to learn what this means, 'Mercy I desire and not sacrifice;' for I did not come to call the righteous but sinners." 14 Then the disciples of John come to him saying, "Why do we and the Pharisees fast a lot, but your disciples do not fast?" 15 And Jesus said to them, "Are the friends of the groom able to mourn as long as the groom is with them? [No!]. But days shall come when the groom may be taken away, and then they shall fast. 16 Now no one puts a patch of new cloth on an old garment; for its repair rips away from the garment, and a worse tear appears. 17 Neither do they put new wine in old wineskins; otherwise, the wineskins burst, and the wine is spilled and the wineskins are destroyed; but they put new wine in new wineskins, and both are preserved."

Matthew 9:18-27

[18] As he was speaking these things to them behold a certain ruler, coming, was kneeling down before him saying this; "My daughter just died; but come to lay your hand upon her, and she shall live." [19] And getting up Jesus and his disciples followed him. [20] And behold a woman who suffered a hemorrhage for twelve years, approaching behind him, touched the fringe of his garment; [21] for she was saying to herself, "If only I can touch his robe I shall be saved." [22] But Jesus turning around and seeing her said, "Be of good courage, daughter your faith has saved you." And the woman was saved from that hour. [23] And after Jesus came into the house of the ruler and after seeing the flute players and the agitated crowd he was [24] saying, "Leave, for the girl is not dead but asleep;" and they were ridiculing him. [25] But when the crowd was thrown out, entering in, he grasped her hand, and the girl was raised. [26] And this report went out into all that land. [27] And as Jesus was passing on from there two blind men followed him crying out and saying, "Have mercy on us, Son of David."

[28] Now after coming into the house the blind men came to him, and Jesus says to them, "Do you believe that I am able to do this?" They say to him, "Yes, Lord." [29] Then he touched their eyes saying, "According to your faith let it happen to you." [30] And their eyes were opened. And Jesus admonished them saying, "See to it that no one knows." [31] But they, going out, made him known in all that land. [32] Now as they were going out behold they brought to him a demon possessed and mute man; [33] and after the demon was cast out the mute spoke. And the crowds marveled saying, "Never has something like this been seen in Israel." [34] But the Pharisees were saying, "By the ruler of the demons he casts out the demons." [35] And Jesus was going about all the cities and villages, teaching in their synagogues and preaching the gospel of the kingdom and healing every disease and every malady. [36] Now seeing the crowds he was moved with compassion for them because they were distressed and dejected like sheep not having a shepherd.

Matthew 9:37-10:4

37 τότε λέγει τοῖς μαθηταῖς αὐτοῦ·

Ὁ μὲν θερισμὸς πολύς, οἱ δὲ ἐργάται ὀλίγοι· 38 δεήθητε οὖν τοῦ κυρίου τοῦ θερισμοῦ ὅπως ἐκβάλῃ ἐργάτας εἰς τὸν θερισμὸν αὐτοῦ.

Κεφ. Ι´

10:1 Καὶ προσκαλεσάμενος τοὺς δώδεκα μαθητὰς αὐτοῦ ἔδωκεν αὐτοῖς ἐξουσίαν πνευμάτων ἀκαθάρτων ὥστε ἐκβάλλειν αὐτὰ καὶ θεραπεύειν πᾶσαν νόσον καὶ πᾶσαν μαλακίαν.

2 τῶν δὲ δώδεκα ἀποστόλων τὰ ὀνόματά ἐστιν ταῦτα· πρῶτος Σίμων ὁ λεγόμενος Πέτρος καὶ Ἀνδρέας ὁ ἀδελφὸς αὐτοῦ, Ἰάκωβος ὁ τοῦ Ζεβεδαίου καὶ Ἰωάννης ὁ ἀδελφὸς αὐτοῦ,

3 Φίλιππος καὶ Βαρθολομαῖος, Θωμᾶς καὶ Ματθαῖος ὁ τελώνης,

Ἰάκωβος ὁ τοῦ Ἀλφαίου καὶ Θαδδαῖος, 4 Σίμων ὁ Καναναῖος καὶ Ἰούδας ὁ Ἰσκαριώτης ὁ καὶ παραδοὺς αὐτόν.

37 Then he says to his disciples, "The harvest is plentiful, but the workers few; therefore beseech the Lord of the Harvest that he may send out workers into his harvest." 10:1 And having called his 12 disciples he gave them power over unclean spirits so as to be casting them out and to heal every sickness and every malady. 2 Now the names of the 12 apostles are these; first Simon who is called Peter and Andrew his brother, James of Zebedee and John his brother, 3 Phillip and Bartholomew, Thomas and Matthew the tax collector, James of Alpheus and Thaddeus, 4 Simon the Zealot and Judas Iscariot who even betrayed him.

Matthew 10:5-25

5 Τούτους τοὺς δώδεκα ἀπέστειλεν ὁ Ἰησοῦς παραγγείλας αὐτοῖς λέγων·

Εἰς ὁδὸν ἐθνῶν μὴ ἀπέλθητε καὶ εἰς πόλιν Σαμαριτῶν μὴ εἰσέλθητε· 6 πορεύεσθε δὲ μᾶλλον πρὸς τὰ πρόβατα τὰ ἀπολωλότα οἴκου Ἰσραήλ. 7 πορευόμενοι δὲ κηρύσσετε λέγοντες ὅτι Ἤγγικεν ἡ βασιλεία τῶν οὐρανῶν. 8 ἀσθενοῦντας θεραπεύετε, νεκροὺς ἐγείρετε, λεπροὺς καθαρίζετε, δαιμόνια ἐκβάλλετε· δωρεὰν ἐλάβετε, δωρεὰν δότε. 9 μὴ κτήσησθε χρυσὸν μηδὲ ἄργυρον μηδὲ χαλκὸν εἰς τὰς ζώνας ὑμῶν, 10 μὴ πήραν εἰς ὁδὸν μηδὲ δύο χιτῶνας μηδὲ ὑποδήματα μηδὲ ῥάβδον· ἄξιος γὰρ ὁ ἐργάτης τῆς τροφῆς αὐτοῦ. 11 εἰς ἣν δ' ἂν πόλιν ἢ κώμην εἰσέλθητε, ἐξετάσατε τίς ἐν αὐτῇ ἄξιός ἐστιν· κἀκεῖ μείνατε ἕως ἂν ἐξέλθητε. 12 εἰσερχόμενοι δὲ εἰς τὴν οἰκίαν ἀσπάσασθε αὐτήν· 13 καὶ ἐὰν μὲν ᾖ ἡ οἰκία ἀξία, ἐλθάτω ἡ εἰρήνη ὑμῶν ἐπ' αὐτήν· ἐὰν δὲ μὴ ᾖ ἀξία, ἡ εἰρήνη ὑμῶν πρὸς ὑμᾶς ἐπιστραφήτω. 14 καὶ ὃς ἂν μὴ δέξηται ὑμᾶς μηδὲ ἀκούσῃ τοὺς λόγους ὑμῶν, ἐξερχόμενοι ἔξω τῆς οἰκίας ἢ τῆς πόλεως ἐκείνης ἐκτινάξατε τὸν κονιορτὸν τῶν ποδῶν ὑμῶν. 15 ἀμὴν λέγω ὑμῖν, ἀνεκτότερον ἔσται γῇ Σοδόμων καὶ Γομόρρων ἐν ἡμέρᾳ κρίσεως ἢ τῇ πόλει ἐκείνῃ. 16 Ἰδοὺ ἐγὼ ἀποστέλλω ὑμᾶς ὡς πρόβατα ἐν μέσῳ λύκων· γίνεσθε οὖν φρόνιμοι ὡς οἱ ὄφεις καὶ ἀκέραιοι ὡς αἱ περιστεραί. 17 προσέχετε δὲ ἀπὸ τῶν ἀνθρώπων· παραδώσουσιν γὰρ ὑμᾶς εἰς συνέδρια, καὶ ἐν ταῖς συναγωγαῖς αὐτῶν μαστιγώσουσιν ὑμᾶς· 18 καὶ ἐπὶ ἡγεμόνας δὲ καὶ βασιλεῖς ἀχθήσεσθε ἕνεκεν ἐμοῦ εἰς μαρτύριον αὐτοῖς καὶ τοῖς ἔθνεσιν. 19 ὅταν δὲ παραδῶσιν ὑμᾶς, μὴ μεριμνήσητε πῶς ἢ τί λαλήσητε· δοθήσεται γὰρ ὑμῖν ἐν ἐκείνῃ τῇ ὥρᾳ τί λαλήσητε· 20 οὐ γὰρ ὑμεῖς ἐστε οἱ λαλοῦντες ἀλλὰ τὸ πνεῦμα τοῦ πατρὸς ὑμῶν τὸ λαλοῦν ἐν ὑμῖν. 21 παραδώσει δὲ ἀδελφὸς ἀδελφὸν εἰς θάνατον καὶ πατὴρ τέκνον, καὶ ἐπαναστήσονται τέκνα ἐπὶ γονεῖς καὶ θανατώσουσιν αὐτούς. 22 καὶ ἔσεσθε μισούμενοι ὑπὸ πάντων διὰ τὸ ὄνομά μου· ὁ δὲ ὑπομείνας εἰς τέλος οὗτος σωθήσεται. 23 ὅταν δὲ διώκωσιν ὑμᾶς ἐν τῇ πόλει ταύτῃ, φεύγετε εἰς τὴν ἑτέραν· ἀμὴν γὰρ λέγω ὑμῖν, οὐ μὴ τελέσητε τὰς πόλεις τοῦ Ἰσραὴλ ἕως ἂν ἔλθῃ ὁ υἱὸς τοῦ ἀνθρώπου. 24 Οὐκ ἔστιν μαθητὴς ὑπὲρ τὸν διδάσκαλον οὐδὲ δοῦλος ὑπὲρ τὸν κύριον αὐτοῦ. 25 ἀρκετὸν τῷ μαθητῇ ἵνα γένηται ὡς ὁ διδάσκαλος αὐτοῦ, καὶ ὁ δοῦλος ὡς ὁ κύριος αὐτοῦ. εἰ τὸν οἰκοδεσπότην Βεελζεβοὺλ ἐπεκάλεσαν, πόσῳ μᾶλλον τοὺς οἰκιακοὺς αὐτοῦ.

⁵ These 12 Jesus sent out charging them saying, "On the road of the Gentiles do not go and into a Samaritan city do not enter; ⁶ but rather go to the lost sheep of the house of Israel. ⁷ Now go to preach saying this: 'The Kingdom of the Heavens is near.' ⁸ Heal those who are ill, raise the dead, cleanse people with skin disease, cast out demons; freely you received, freely give. ⁹ Do not acquire gold nor silver nor copper [to put] in your belts, ¹⁰ nor a bag for the journey nor two tunics nor sandals nor a staff; for the worker is worth his food. ¹¹ So, into whichever city or town you enter, seek someone in it who is worthy; and remain there until you go. ¹² Now, as you enter into the house greet it; ¹³ and if indeed the house is worthy, bring your peace upon it but if it is not worthy, let your peace return to you. ¹⁴ And whoever does not receive you nor listens to your words, leaving the house or that city, shake the dust off your feet. ¹⁵ Amen! I am saying to you, it shall be more tolerable in the land of Sodom and Gomorrah on the Day of Judgment than in that city. ¹⁶ Behold I am sending you as sheep in the midst of wolves; therefore, be wise as serpents and innocent as doves. ¹⁷ But beware of people; for they shall hand you over to local councils and in their synagogues they shall scourge you; ¹⁸ and before rulers but also kings you shall be brought on account of me as a witness to them and the nations. ¹⁹ But whenever they may hand you over, do not worry about how or what to say; for you shall be given in that hour what you should say; ²⁰ for you are not the ones speaking but [it is] the Spirit of our Father which is speaking in you. ²¹ So brother shall hand over brother to death and a father a child, and children shall rise up against parents and kill them. ²² And you shall be hated by all because of my name; but the one who endures to the end he shall be saved. ²³ But when they persecute you in this city, flee to another; for Amen! I am saying to you, you will certainly not complete [going to] all the cities of Israel before the Son of Man comes. ²⁴ A disciple is not above the teacher nor a slave over his master. ²⁵ It is sufficient for the disciple that he might become like his teacher, and the slave as his master.

Matthew 10:26-42

²⁶ Μὴ οὖν φοβηθῆτε αὐτούς· οὐδὲν γάρ ἐστιν κεκαλυμμένον ὃ οὐκ ἀποκαλυφθήσεται, καὶ κρυπτὸν ὃ οὐ γνωσθήσεται. ²⁷ ὃ λέγω ὑμῖν ἐν τῇ σκοτίᾳ, εἴπατε ἐν τῷ φωτί· καὶ ὃ εἰς τὸ οὖς ἀκούετε, κηρύξατε ἐπὶ τῶν δωμάτων. ²⁸ καὶ μὴ φοβεῖσθε ἀπὸ τῶν ἀποκτεννόντων τὸ σῶμα τὴν δὲ ψυχὴν μὴ δυναμένων ἀποκτεῖναι· φοβεῖσθε δὲ μᾶλλον τὸν δυνάμενον καὶ ψυχὴν καὶ σῶμα ἀπολέσαι ἐν γεέννῃ. ²⁹ οὐχὶ δύο στρουθία ἀσσαρίου πωλεῖται; καὶ ἓν ἐξ αὐτῶν οὐ πεσεῖται ἐπὶ τὴν γῆν ἄνευ τοῦ πατρὸς ὑμῶν. ³⁰ ὑμῶν δὲ καὶ αἱ τρίχες τῆς κεφαλῆς πᾶσαι ἠριθμημέναι εἰσίν. ³¹ μὴ οὖν φοβεῖσθε· πολλῶν στρουθίων διαφέρετε ὑμεῖς. ³² Πᾶς οὖν ὅστις ὁμολογήσει ἐν ἐμοὶ ἔμπροσθεν τῶν ἀνθρώπων, ὁμολογήσω κἀγὼ ἐν αὐτῷ ἔμπροσθεν τοῦ πατρός μου τοῦ ἐν οὐρανοῖς· ³³ ὅστις δ' ἂν ἀρνήσηταί με ἔμπροσθεν τῶν ἀνθρώπων, ἀρνήσομαι κἀγὼ αὐτὸν ἔμπροσθεν τοῦ πατρός μου τοῦ ἐν οὐρανοῖς. ³⁴ Μὴ νομίσητε ὅτι ἦλθον βαλεῖν εἰρήνην ἐπὶ τὴν γῆν· οὐκ ἦλθον βαλεῖν εἰρήνην ἀλλὰ μάχαιραν. ³⁵ ἦλθον γὰρ διχάσαι ἄνθρωπον κατὰ τοῦ πατρὸς αὐτοῦ καὶ θυγατέρα κατὰ τῆς μητρὸς αὐτῆς καὶ νύμφην κατὰ τῆς πενθερᾶς αὐτῆς, ³⁶ καὶ ἐχθροὶ τοῦ ἀνθρώπου οἱ οἰκιακοὶ αὐτοῦ. ³⁷ ὁ φιλῶν πατέρα ἢ μητέρα ὑπὲρ ἐμὲ οὐκ ἔστιν μου ἄξιος· καὶ ὁ φιλῶν υἱὸν ἢ θυγατέρα ὑπὲρ ἐμὲ οὐκ ἔστιν μου ἄξιος· ³⁸ καὶ ὃς οὐ λαμβάνει τὸν σταυρὸν αὐτοῦ καὶ ἀκολουθεῖ ὀπίσω μου, οὐκ ἔστιν μου ἄξιος. ³⁹ ὁ εὑρὼν τὴν ψυχὴν αὐτοῦ ἀπολέσει αὐτήν, καὶ ὁ ἀπολέσας τὴν ψυχὴν αὐτοῦ ἕνεκεν ἐμοῦ εὑρήσει αὐτήν. ⁴⁰ Ὁ δεχόμενος ὑμᾶς ἐμὲ δέχεται, καὶ ὁ ἐμὲ δεχόμενος δέχεται τὸν ἀποστείλαντά με. ⁴¹ ὁ δεχόμενος προφήτην εἰς ὄνομα προφήτου μισθὸν προφήτου λήμψεται, καὶ ὁ δεχόμενος δίκαιον εἰς ὄνομα δικαίου μισθὸν δικαίου λήμψεται. ⁴² καὶ ὃς ἂν ποτίσῃ ἕνα τῶν μικρῶν τούτων ποτήριον ψυχροῦ μόνον εἰς ὄνομα μαθητοῦ, ἀμὴν λέγω ὑμῖν, οὐ μὴ ἀπολέσῃ τὸν μισθὸν αὐτοῦ.

²⁶ "Then do not be afraid of them; for there is nothing concealed which shall not be revealed, and hidden which shall not be known. ²⁷ That which I am saying to you in darkness, speak in the light; and that which you hear with the ear, proclaim on the rooftops. ²⁸ And do not be afraid of those who kill the body but are not able to kill the soul; but fear rather the one who is able to destroy both soul and body in Gehenna. ²⁹ Are not two sparrows sold for an assarion? [Yes!] And one of them shall not fall unto the ground without your Father. ³⁰ So also all the hairs of your head are numbered. ³¹ Do not be afraid; you are worth much more than sparrows. ³² Everyone then who professes me before people, I also shall profess before my Father who is in the heavens; ³³ but whoever denies me before people, I shall also deny before my Father who is in the heavens. ³⁴ Do not think that I came to bring peace on the earth; I came not to bring peace but a sword. ³⁵ For I came to divide a man against his father and a daughter against her mother and a bride against her mother-in-law, ³⁶ and a man's enemies [will be] his own household. ³⁷ The one who loves a father or mother more than me is not worthy of me; and the one who loves a son or a daughter more than me is not worthy of me; ³⁸ and the one who does not take his cross and follows after me, is not worthy of me. ³⁹ The one who finds his life shall lose it, and the one who loses his life on account of me shall find it. ⁴⁰ The one who receives you receives me, and the one who receives me receives the one who sent me. ⁴¹ The one who receives a prophet because he is a prophet shall receive a prophet's reward, and the one who receives a righteous person because he is righteous shall receive a righteous person's reward. ⁴² And whoever gives to one of the least of these even a cold cup to drink in the name of a disciple, Amen! I am saying to you, he shall certainly not lose his reward."

Matthew 11:1-15

Κεφ. ΙΑ΄

11:1 Καὶ ἐγένετο ὅτε ἐτέλεσεν ὁ Ἰησοῦς διατάσσων τοῖς δώδεκα μαθηταῖς αὐτοῦ, μετέβη ἐκεῖθεν τοῦ διδάσκειν καὶ κηρύσσειν ἐν ταῖς πόλεσιν αὐτῶν.

2 Ὁ δὲ Ἰωάννης ἀκούσας ἐν τῷ δεσμωτηρίῳ τὰ ἔργα τοῦ χριστοῦ πέμψας διὰ τῶν μαθητῶν αὐτοῦ **3** εἶπεν αὐτῷ· **4** καὶ ἀποκριθεὶς ὁ Ἰησοῦς εἶπεν αὐτοῖς·

Σὺ εἶ ὁ ἐρχόμενος ἢ ἕτερον προσδοκῶμεν;

Πορευθέντες ἀπαγγείλατε Ἰωάννῃ ἃ ἀκούετε καὶ βλέπετε· **5** τυφλοὶ ἀναβλέπουσιν καὶ χωλοὶ περιπατοῦσιν, λεπροὶ καθαρίζονται καὶ κωφοὶ ἀκούουσιν, καὶ νεκροὶ ἐγείρονται καὶ πτωχοὶ εὐαγγελίζονται· **6** καὶ μακάριός ἐστιν ὃς ἐὰν μὴ σκανδαλισθῇ ἐν ἐμοί.

7 Τούτων δὲ πορευομένων ἤρξατο ὁ Ἰησοῦς λέγειν τοῖς ὄχλοις περὶ Ἰωάννου·

Τί ἐξήλθατε εἰς τὴν ἔρημον θεάσασθαι; κάλαμον ὑπὸ ἀνέμου σαλευόμενον; **8** ἀλλὰ τί ἐξήλθατε ἰδεῖν; ἄνθρωπον ἐν μαλακοῖς ἠμφιεσμένον; ἰδοὺ οἱ τὰ μαλακὰ φοροῦντες ἐν τοῖς οἴκοις τῶν βασιλέων εἰσίν. **9** ἀλλὰ τί ἐξήλθατε; προφήτην ἰδεῖν; ναί, λέγω ὑμῖν, καὶ περισσότερον προφήτου. **10** οὗτός ἐστιν περὶ οὗ γέγραπται· Ἰδοὺ ἐγὼ ἀποστέλλω τὸν ἄγγελόν μου πρὸ προσώπου σου, ὃς κατασκευάσει τὴν ὁδόν σου ἔμπροσθέν σου. **11** ἀμὴν λέγω ὑμῖν, οὐκ ἐγήγερται ἐν γεννητοῖς γυναικῶν μείζων Ἰωάννου τοῦ βαπτιστοῦ· ὁ δὲ μικρότερος ἐν τῇ βασιλείᾳ τῶν οὐρανῶν μείζων αὐτοῦ ἐστιν. **12** ἀπὸ δὲ τῶν ἡμερῶν Ἰωάννου τοῦ βαπτιστοῦ ἕως ἄρτι ἡ βασιλεία τῶν οὐρανῶν βιάζεται, καὶ βιασταὶ ἁρπάζουσιν αὐτήν. **13** πάντες γὰρ οἱ προφῆται καὶ ὁ νόμος ἕως Ἰωάννου ἐπροφήτευσαν· **14** καὶ εἰ θέλετε δέξασθαι, αὐτός ἐστιν Ἠλίας ὁ μέλλων ἔρχεσθαι. **15** ὁ ἔχων ὦτα ἀκουέτω.

11:1 And it happened when Jesus finished commanding his 12 disciples, he departed from there to teach and preach in their cities. **2** Now John, having heard in prison about the works of the Messiah, having sent [a word] through his disciples, **3** said to him, "Are you the coming one or should we look for another?" **4** And answering Jesus said to them, "Go to announce to John that which you hear and see; **5** blind receive sight and lame walk, people with skin diseases are cleansed and deaf hear, and dead are raised and poor are brought good news; **6** and blessed is he if he is not repelled by me." **7** But as these [people] are leaving Jesus began to speak to the crowds concerning John, "What did you go out into the wilderness to behold? A reed shaken by the wind? **8** But what did you go out to see? A man clothed in soft clothes? Behold those who wear soft clothes are in the houses of kings. **9** But what did you go out to? To see a prophet? Yes, I tell you, and more than a prophet. **10** This is the one concerning whom it has been written; 'Behold I am sending my messenger before you, who shall prepare your way before you.' **11** Amen! I am saying to you, there has not risen one born among women greater than John the Baptist; but the least in the Kingdom of the Heavens is greater than him. **12** But from the days of John the Baptist until now the Kingdom of the Heavens suffers violence, and violent men seize it. **13** For all the prophets and the Law prophesied until John; **14** and if you are willing to accept [it], he is Elijah who is about to come. The one who has ears, listen!"

Matthew 11:16-24

16 Τίνι δὲ ὁμοιώσω τὴν γενεὰν ταύτην; ὁμοία ἐστὶν παιδίοις καθημένοις ἐν ταῖς ἀγοραῖς ἃ προσφωνοῦντα τοῖς ἑτέροις 17 λέγουσιν· Ηὐλήσαμεν ὑμῖν καὶ οὐκ ὠρχήσασθε· ἐθρηνήσαμεν καὶ οὐκ ἐκόψασθε· 18 ἦλθεν γὰρ Ἰωάννης μήτε ἐσθίων μήτε πίνων, καὶ λέγουσιν· Δαιμόνιον ἔχει· 19 ἦλθεν ὁ υἱὸς τοῦ ἀνθρώπου ἐσθίων καὶ πίνων, καὶ λέγουσιν· Ἰδοὺ ἄνθρωπος φάγος καὶ οἰνοπότης, τελωνῶν φίλος καὶ ἁμαρτωλῶν. καὶ ἐδικαιώθη ἡ σοφία ἀπὸ τῶν ἔργων αὐτῆς.

20 Τότε ἤρξατο ὀνειδίζειν τὰς πόλεις ἐν αἷς ἐγένοντο αἱ πλεῖσται δυνάμεις αὐτοῦ, ὅτι οὐ μετενόησαν·

21 Οὐαί σοι, Χοραζίν· οὐαί σοι, Βηθσαϊδά· ὅτι εἰ ἐν Τύρῳ καὶ Σιδῶνι ἐγένοντο αἱ δυνάμεις αἱ γενόμεναι ἐν ὑμῖν, πάλαι ἂν ἐν σάκκῳ καὶ σποδῷ μετενόησαν. 22 πλὴν λέγω ὑμῖν, Τύρῳ καὶ Σιδῶνι ἀνεκτότερον ἔσται ἐν ἡμέρᾳ κρίσεως ἢ ὑμῖν. 23 καὶ σύ, Καφαρναούμ, ‘μὴ ἕως οὐρανοῦ ὑψωθήσῃ; ἕως ᾅδου καταβήσῃ· ὅτι εἰ ἐν Σοδόμοις ἐγενήθησαν αἱ δυνάμεις αἱ γενόμεναι ἐν σοί, ἔμεινεν ἂν μέχρι τῆς σήμερον. 24 πλὴν λέγω ὑμῖν ὅτι γῇ Σοδόμων ἀνεκτότερον ἔσται ἐν ἡμέρᾳ κρίσεως ἢ σοί.

[16] "Now to what shall I compare this generation? It is like children sitting in the agoras calling out to others [17] saying, 'We played the flute for you and you did not dance; we sang a dirge and you did not mourn;' [18] For John came neither eating nor drinking, and they say, 'He has a demon;' [19] the Son of Man came eating and drinking, and you say, 'Behold a man, a glutton and drunkard, a friend of tax collectors and sinners. And wisdom is vindicated by her deeds.'" [20] Then he began to reproach the cities in which most of his deeds of powers occurred, because they did not repent; [21] "Woe to you, Chorazin! Woe to you, Bethsaida! Because if the deeds of power had occurred in Tyre and Sidon that happened in you, they would have repented long ago in sackcloth and ashes. [22] However, I am saying to you, 'In Tyre and Sidon it shall be more bearable on judgment day than for you.' [23] And you, Capernaum, shall you be exalted as far as Heaven? [No!] You shall descend as far as Hades; because if the deeds of power had occurred in Sodom that happened in you, it would have remained until today. [24] Nevertheless, I am saying to you that it shall be more bearable in the land of Sodom on judgment day than for you."

Matthew 11:25-12:4

25 Ἐν ἐκείνῳ τῷ καιρῷ ἀποκριθεὶς ὁ Ἰησοῦς εἶπεν·

Ἐξομολογοῦμαί σοι, πάτερ κύριε τοῦ οὐρανοῦ καὶ τῆς γῆς, ὅτι ἔκρυψας ταῦτα ἀπὸ σοφῶν καὶ συνετῶν, καὶ ἀπεκάλυψας αὐτὰ νηπίοις· 26 ναί, ὁ πατήρ, ὅτι οὕτως εὐδοκία ἐγένετο ἔμπροσθέν σου. 27 Πάντα μοι παρεδόθη ὑπὸ τοῦ πατρός μου, καὶ οὐδεὶς ἐπιγινώσκει τὸν υἱὸν εἰ μὴ ὁ πατήρ, οὐδὲ τὸν πατέρα τις ἐπιγινώσκει εἰ μὴ ὁ υἱὸς καὶ ᾧ ἐὰν βούληται ὁ υἱὸς ἀποκαλύψαι.

28 Δεῦτε πρός με πάντες οἱ κοπιῶντες καὶ πεφορτισμένοι, κἀγὼ ἀναπαύσω ὑμᾶς. 29 ἄρατε τὸν ζυγόν μου ἐφ'ὑμᾶς καὶ μάθετε ἀπ' ἐμοῦ, ὅτι πραΰς εἰμι καὶ ταπεινὸς τῇ καρδίᾳ, καὶ εὑρήσετε ἀνάπαυσιν ταῖς ψυχαῖς ὑμῶν· 30 ὁ γὰρ ζυγός μου χρηστὸς καὶ τὸ φορτίον μου ἐλαφρόν ἐστιν.

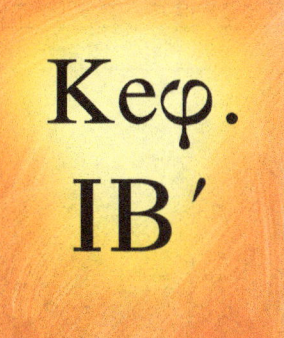

Κεφ. ΙΒ΄

12:1 Ἐν ἐκείνῳ τῷ καιρῷ ἐπορεύθη ὁ Ἰησοῦς τοῖς σάββασιν διὰ τῶν σπορίμων· οἱ δὲ μαθηταὶ αὐτοῦ ἐπείνασαν καὶ ἤρξαντο τίλλειν στάχυας καὶ ἐσθίειν.

2 οἱ δὲ Φαρισαῖοι ἰδόντες εἶπαν αὐτῷ·   3 ὁ δὲ εἶπεν αὐτοῖς·

Ἰδοὺ οἱ μαθηταί σου ποιοῦσιν ὃ οὐκ ἔξεστιν ποιεῖν ἐν σαββάτῳ.

Οὐκ ἀνέγνωτε τί ἐποίησεν Δαυὶδ ὅτε ἐπείνασεν καὶ οἱ μετ' αὐτοῦ; 4 πῶς εἰσῆλθεν εἰς τὸν οἶκον τοῦ θεοῦ καὶ τοὺς ἄρτους τῆς προθέσεως ἔφαγον, ὃ οὐκ ἐξὸν ἦν αὐτῷ φαγεῖν οὐδὲ τοῖς μετ' αὐτοῦ, εἰ μὴ τοῖς ἱερεῦσιν μόνοις;

25 At that moment, answering, Jesus said, "I praise you, Father, Lord of heaven and the earth, because you have hidden these things from the wise and clever, and revealed them to children; 26 yes, Father, because thus it was well-pleasing before you. 27 All things have been handed over to me by my Father, and no one knows the Son except the Father, nor does anyone know the Father except the Son and anyone to whom the Son wishes to reveal [Him]." 28 "Come to me all who are laboring and burdened, and I shall give you rest. 29 Take my yoke upon you and learn from me, because I am gentle and humble in heart, and you shall find rest for yourselves; 30 for my yoke is good and my burden is light." 12:1 At that time Jesus went through the grain fields on the Sabbath; but his disciples were hungry and began to pluck heads of grain and to eat. 2 Now the Pharisees seeing [it] said to him, "Behold your disciples do that which is not permitted to do on the Sabbath." 3 But he said to them, "Have you not read what David did when he was hungry and those with him? 4 How he entered into the house of God and ate the bread of presentation, which was not lawful for him to eat nor those with him, except the priests alone?" [Surely, yes!]

Matthew 12:5-14

5 ἢ οὐκ ἀνέγνωτε ἐν τῷ νόμῳ ὅτι τοῖς σάββασιν οἱ ἱερεῖς ἐν τῷ ἱερῷ τὸ σάββατον βεβηλοῦσιν καὶ ἀναίτιοί εἰσιν; 6 λέγω δὲ ὑμῖν ὅτι τοῦ ἱεροῦ μεῖζόν ἐστιν ὧδε. 7 εἰ δὲ ἐγνώκειτε τί ἐστιν·

Ἔλεος θέλω καὶ οὐ θυσίαν,

οὐκ ἂν κατεδικάσατε τοὺς ἀναιτίους. 8 κύριος γάρ ἐστιν τοῦ σαββάτου ὁ υἱὸς τοῦ ἀνθρώπου.

9 Καὶ μεταβὰς ἐκεῖθεν ἦλθεν εἰς τὴν συναγωγὴν αὐτῶν·

Εἰ ἔξεστι τοῖς σάββασιν θεραπεύειν;

10 καὶ ἰδοὺ ἄνθρωπος χεῖρα ἔχων ξηράν. καὶ ἐπηρώτησαν αὐτὸν λέγοντες·

ἵνα κατηγορήσωσιν αὐτοῦ.

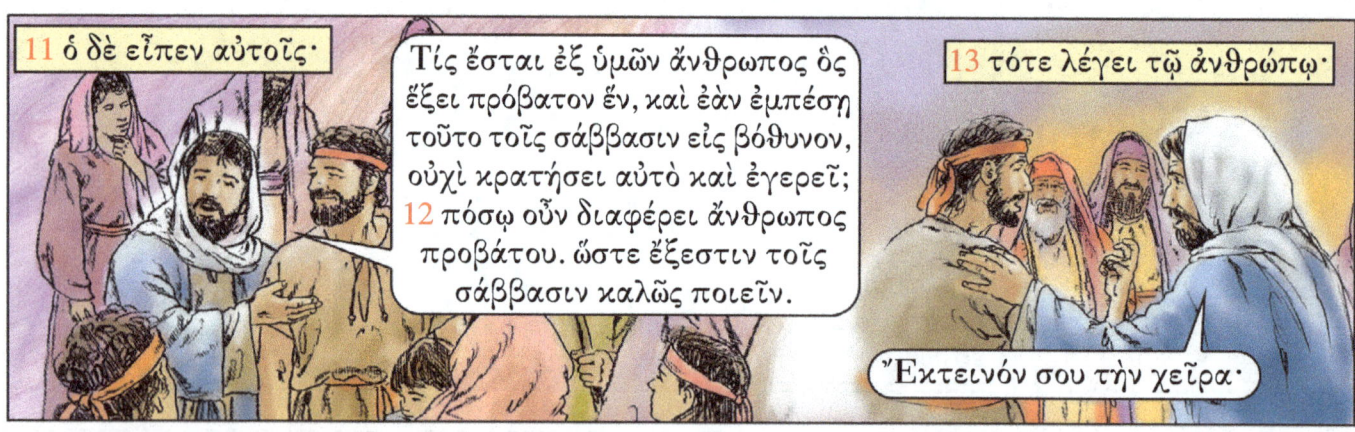

11 ὁ δὲ εἶπεν αὐτοῖς·

Τίς ἔσται ἐξ ὑμῶν ἄνθρωπος ὃς ἕξει πρόβατον ἕν, καὶ ἐὰν ἐμπέσῃ τοῦτο τοῖς σάββασιν εἰς βόθυνον, οὐχὶ κρατήσει αὐτὸ καὶ ἐγερεῖ; 12 πόσῳ οὖν διαφέρει ἄνθρωπος προβάτου. ὥστε ἔξεστιν τοῖς σάββασιν καλῶς ποιεῖν.

13 τότε λέγει τῷ ἀνθρώπῳ·

Ἔκτεινόν σου τὴν χεῖρα·

καὶ ἐξέτεινεν, καὶ ἀπεκατεστάθη ὑγιὴς ὡς ἡ ἄλλη.

14 ἐξελθόντες δὲ οἱ Φαρισαῖοι συμβούλιον ἔλαβον κατ' αὐτοῦ ὅπως αὐτὸν ἀπολέσωσιν.

5 "Or have you not read in the Law that the priests on the Sabbath in the Temple profane the Sabbath and are still innocent? [Surely, yes!] 6 Now I am saying to you that something greater than the Temple is here. 7 So, if you had known what this means; 'Mercy I desire and not sacrifice,' you would not have condemned the innocent. 8 For the Son of Man is lord of the Sabbath." 9 And departing from there he came into their synagogue; 10 and behold, a man having a withered hand! And they questioned him saying, "Is it lawful to heal on the Sabbath?" In order that they might accuse him. 11 So he said to them, "Which person from among you would there be who would have one sheep, and if this one were to fall on the Sabbath into a pit, would he not grasp it and lift it up? [Yes!] 12 How much more valuable, then, is a person than a sheep! Therefore, it is lawful on the Sabbath to do good." 13 Then he says to the man, "Stretch forth your hand" and he stretched forth, and it was restored whole just as the other. 14 But leaving the Pharisees called a council against him in order that they might destroy him.

Matthew 12:29-37

29 ἢ πῶς δύναταί τις εἰσελθεῖν εἰς τὴν οἰκίαν τοῦ ἰσχυροῦ καὶ τὰ σκεύη αὐτοῦ ἁρπάσαι, ἐὰν μὴ πρῶτον δήσῃ τὸν ἰσχυρόν; καὶ τότε τὴν οἰκίαν αὐτοῦ διαρπάσει. 30 ὁ μὴ ὢν μετ' ἐμοῦ κατ' ἐμοῦ ἐστιν, καὶ ὁ μὴ συνάγων μετ' ἐμοῦ σκορπίζει. 31 διὰ τοῦτο λέγω ὑμῖν, πᾶσα ἁμαρτία καὶ βλασφημία ἀφεθήσεται τοῖς ἀνθρώποις, ἡ δὲ τοῦ πνεύματος βλασφημία οὐκ ἀφεθήσεται. 32 καὶ ὃς ἐὰν εἴπῃ λόγον κατὰ τοῦ υἱοῦ τοῦ ἀνθρώπου, ἀφεθήσεται αὐτῷ· ὃς δ' ἂν εἴπῃ κατὰ τοῦ πνεύματος τοῦ ἁγίου, οὐκ ἀφεθήσεται αὐτῷ οὔτε ἐν τούτῳ τῷ αἰῶνι οὔτε ἐν τῷ μέλλοντι.

33 Ἢ ποιήσατε τὸ δένδρον καλὸν καὶ τὸν καρπὸν αὐτοῦ καλόν, ἢ ποιήσατε τὸ δένδρον σαπρὸν καὶ τὸν καρπὸν αὐτοῦ σαπρόν· ἐκ γὰρ τοῦ καρποῦ τὸ δένδρον γινώσκεται. 34 γεννήματα ἐχιδνῶν, πῶς δύνασθε ἀγαθὰ λαλεῖν πονηροὶ ὄντες; ἐκ γὰρ τοῦ περισσεύματος τῆς καρδίας τὸ στόμα λαλεῖ. 35 ὁ ἀγαθὸς ἄνθρωπος ἐκ τοῦ ἀγαθοῦ θησαυροῦ ἐκβάλλει ἀγαθά, καὶ ὁ πονηρὸς ἄνθρωπος ἐκ τοῦ πονηροῦ θησαυροῦ ἐκβάλλει πονηρά. 36 λέγω δὲ ὑμῖν ὅτι πᾶν ῥῆμα ἀργὸν ὃ λαλήσουσιν οἱ ἄνθρωποι, ἀποδώσουσιν περὶ αὐτοῦ λόγον ἐν ἡμέρᾳ κρίσεως· 37 ἐκ γὰρ τῶν λόγων σου δικαιωθήσῃ, καὶ ἐκ τῶν λόγων σου καταδικασθήσῃ.

29 "Or how is anyone able to enter into the house of a strong man and seize his goods, unless he first tied up the strong man? And then he shall plunder his house. 30 The one who is not with me is against me, and the one who is not gathering with me scatters. 31 Because of this I am saying to you, 'Every sin and blasphemy shall be forgiven to people, but blasphemy of the Holy Spirit shall not be forgiven.' 32 And if someone speaks a word against the Son of Man, it shall be forgiven him; but if someone speaks against the Holy Spirit, it shall not be forgiven him neither in this age nor in the coming one. 33 Either make the tree good and its fruit good, or make the tree rotten and its fruit rotten; for the tree is known by its fruit. 34 Brood of vipers! How are you able to speak good things being evil? For out of the abundance of the heart the mouth speaks. 35 The good person brings out good from the good treasure chest, and the evil person brings out evil from the evil treasure chest. 36 But I am saying to you that every useless word that people shall speak, they shall render account for it on judgment day; 37 for by your words you shall be justified, and by your words you shall be condemned."

Matthew 12:38-45

38 Τότε ἀπεκρίθησαν αὐτῷ τινες τῶν γραμματέων καὶ Φαρισαίων λέγοντες·

Διδάσκαλε, θέλομεν ἀπὸ σοῦ σημεῖον ἰδεῖν.

39 ὁ δὲ ἀποκριθεὶς εἶπεν αὐτοῖς·

Γενεὰ πονηρὰ καὶ μοιχαλὶς σημεῖον ἐπιζητεῖ, καὶ σημεῖον οὐ δοθήσεται αὐτῇ εἰ μὴ τὸ σημεῖον Ἰωνᾶ τοῦ προφήτου. 40 ὥσπερ γὰρ ἦν Ἰωνᾶς ἐν τῇ κοιλίᾳ τοῦ κήτους τρεῖς ἡμέρας καὶ τρεῖς νύκτας, οὕτως ἔσται ὁ υἱὸς τοῦ ἀνθρώπου ἐν τῇ καρδίᾳ τῆς γῆς τρεῖς ἡμέρας καὶ τρεῖς νύκτας. 41 ἄνδρες Νινευῖται ἀναστήσονται ἐν τῇ κρίσει μετὰ τῆς γενεᾶς ταύτης καὶ κατακρινοῦσιν αὐτήν· ὅτι μετενόησαν εἰς τὸ κήρυγμα Ἰωνᾶ, καὶ ἰδοὺ πλεῖον Ἰωνᾶ ὧδε. 42 βασίλισσα νότου ἐγερθήσεται ἐν τῇ κρίσει μετὰ τῆς γενεᾶς ταύτης καὶ κατακρινεῖ αὐτήν· ὅτι ἦλθεν ἐκ τῶν περάτων τῆς γῆς ἀκοῦσαι τὴν σοφίαν Σολομῶνος, καὶ ἰδοὺ πλεῖον Σολομῶνος ὧδε.

43 Ὅταν δὲ τὸ ἀκάθαρτον πνεῦμα ἐξέλθῃ ἀπὸ τοῦ ἀνθρώπου, διέρχεται δι᾽ ἀνύδρων τόπων ζητοῦν ἀνάπαυσιν, καὶ οὐχ εὑρίσκει. 44 τότε λέγει· Εἰς τὸν οἶκόν μου ἐπιστρέψω ὅθεν ἐξῆλθον· καὶ ἐλθὸν εὑρίσκει σχολάζοντα σεσαρωμένον καὶ κεκοσμημένον. 45 τότε πορεύεται καὶ παραλαμβάνει μεθ᾽ ἑαυτοῦ ἑπτὰ ἕτερα πνεύματα πονηρότερα ἑαυτοῦ, καὶ εἰσελθόντα κατοικεῖ ἐκεῖ· καὶ γίνεται τὰ ἔσχατα τοῦ ἀνθρώπου ἐκείνου χείρονα τῶν πρώτων. οὕτως ἔσται καὶ τῇ γενεᾷ ταύτῃ τῇ πονηρᾷ.

38 Then some of the scribes and Pharisees answered back saying, "Teacher, we wish to see a sign from you." 39 So answering back he said to them, "An evil and adulterous generation seeks a sign, and a sign shall not be given to it except the sign of Jonah the prophet." 40 For just as Jonah was in the belly of the sea-monster three days and three nights, so the Son of Man shall be in the heart of the earth three days and three nights. 41 Men of Nineveh shall stand in the judgment with this generation and judge it; for they repented by the preaching of Jonah, and behold something greater than Jonah is here. 42 The Queen of the South shall be raised up in the judgment with this generation and condemn it; for she came from a distant land to hear the wisdom of Solomon, and behold something greater than Solomon is here. 43 Now whenever the unclean spirit has gone out from the person, it passes through dry places seeking rest, and does not find it. 44 Then it says, 'To my house shall I return from where I went out;' and going it finds [it] unoccupied swept and adorned. 45 Then it comes and brings with it seven other spirits more evil than itself, and entering in they dwell there; and the last man becomes worse than the first. Thus it shall be even with this evil generation."

Matthew 12:46-13:9

46 Ἔτι δὲ αὐτοῦ λαλοῦντος τοῖς ὄχλοις ἰδοὺ ἡ μήτηρ καὶ οἱ ἀδελφοὶ αὐτοῦ εἱστήκεισαν ἔξω ζητοῦντες αὐτῷ λαλῆσαι. 47 εἶπεν δέ τις αὐτῷ·

Ἰδοὺ ἡ μήτηρ σου καὶ οἱ ἀδελφοί σου ἔξω ἑστήκασιν, ζητοῦντές σοι λαλῆσαι.

48 ὁ δὲ ἀποκριθεὶς εἶπεν τῷ λέγοντι αὐτῷ·

49 καὶ ἐκτείνας τὴν χεῖρα αὐτοῦ ἐπὶ τοὺς μαθητὰς αὐτοῦ εἶπεν·

Τίς ἐστιν ἡ μήτηρ μου, καὶ τίνες εἰσὶν οἱ ἀδελφοί μου;

Ἰδοὺ ἡ μήτηρ μου καὶ οἱ ἀδελφοί μου· 50 ὅστις γὰρ ἂν ποιήσῃ τὸ θέλημα τοῦ πατρός μου τοῦ ἐν οὐρανοῖς, αὐτός μου ἀδελφὸς καὶ ἀδελφὴ καὶ μήτηρ ἐστίν.

Κεφ. ΙΓ΄

13:1 Ἐν τῇ ἡμέρᾳ ἐκείνῃ ἐξελθὼν ὁ Ἰησοῦς τῆς οἰκίας ἐκάθητο παρὰ τὴν θάλασσαν· 2 καὶ συνήχθησαν πρὸς αὐτὸν ὄχλοι πολλοί, ὥστε αὐτὸν εἰς πλοῖον ἐμβάντα καθῆσθαι, καὶ πᾶς ὁ ὄχλος ἐπὶ τὸν αἰγιαλὸν εἱστήκει 3 καὶ ἐλάλησεν αὐτοῖς πολλὰ ἐν παραβολαῖς λέγων·

Ἰδοὺ ἐξῆλθεν ὁ σπείρων τοῦ σπείρειν. 4 καὶ ἐν τῷ σπείρειν αὐτὸν ἃ μὲν ἔπεσεν παρὰ τὴν ὁδόν, καὶ ἐλθόντα τὰ πετεινὰ κατέφαγεν αὐτά. 5 ἄλλα δὲ ἔπεσεν ἐπὶ τὰ πετρώδη ὅπου οὐκ εἶχεν γῆν πολλήν, καὶ εὐθέως ἐξανέτειλεν διὰ τὸ μὴ ἔχειν βάθος γῆς, 6 ἡλίου δὲ ἀνατείλαντος ἐκαυματίσθη καὶ διὰ τὸ μὴ ἔχειν ῥίζαν ἐξηράνθη. 7 ἄλλα δὲ ἔπεσεν ἐπὶ τὰς ἀκάνθας, καὶ ἀνέβησαν αἱ ἄκανθαι καὶ ἔπνιξαν αὐτά. 8 ἄλλα δὲ ἔπεσεν ἐπὶ τὴν γῆν τὴν καλὴν καὶ ἐδίδου καρπόν, ὃ μὲν ἑκατὸν ὃ δὲ ἑξήκοντα ὃ δὲ τριάκοντα. 9 ὁ ἔχων ὦτα ἀκουέτω.

46 But while he was still speaking to the crowds behold his mother and his siblings were standing outside seeking to speak to him. 47 So, someone said to him, "Behold your mother and your siblings stand outside, seeking to speak to you. 48 But answering back he said to the one speaking to him, "Who is my mother, and who are my siblings?" 49 And stretching forth his hand toward his disciples he said, "Behold my mother and my siblings. 50 For whoever does the will of my Father who is in the heavens, such one is my brother and sister and mother." 13:1 On that day after departing the house Jesus was sitting by the lake; 2 and great crowds were gathered around him, with the result that, embarking onto a boat, he sat down, and the entire crowd stood on the shore. 3 And he spoke to them many things in parables saying, "Behold the sower went out to sow. 4 And in his sowing, some fell by the road, and coming the birds ate them. 5 But some fell on rocky places where they were not having much soil, and immediately they sprouted because they did not have depth of soil, 6 but after the sun had risen it was scorched and because it did not have a root it was dried up. 7 But now some fell among thorns, and the thorns grew up and choked them. 8 But now some fell on good soil and was producing fruit, some a hundredfold, some sixty, some thirty. 9 The one who has ears, listen!"

Matthew 13:10-17

10 Καὶ προσελθόντες οἱ μαθηταὶ εἶπαν αὐτῷ·

Διὰ τί ἐν παραβολαῖς λαλεῖς αὐτοῖς;

11 ὁ δὲ ἀποκριθεὶς εἶπεν αὐτοῖς·

Ὅτι ὑμῖν δέδοται γνῶναι τὰ μυστήρια τῆς βασιλείας τῶν οὐρανῶν, ἐκείνοις δὲ οὐ δέδοται. 12 ὅστις γὰρ ἔχει, δοθήσεται αὐτῷ καὶ περισσευθήσεται· ὅστις δὲ οὐκ ἔχει, καὶ ὃ ἔχει ἀρθήσεται ἀπ' αὐτοῦ.

13 διὰ τοῦτο ἐν παραβολαῖς αὐτοῖς λαλῶ, ὅτι βλέποντες οὐ βλέπουσιν καὶ ἀκούοντες οὐκ ἀκούουσιν οὐδὲ συνίουσιν· 14 καὶ ἀναπληροῦται αὐτοῖς ἡ προφητεία Ἠσαΐου ἡ λέγουσα· Ἀκοῇ ἀκούσετε καὶ οὐ μὴ συνῆτε, καὶ βλέποντες βλέψετε καὶ οὐ μὴ ἴδητε. 15 ἐπαχύνθη γὰρ ἡ καρδία τοῦ λαοῦ τούτου, καὶ τοῖς ὠσὶν βαρέως ἤκουσαν, καὶ τοὺς ὀφθαλμοὺς αὐτῶν ἐκάμμυσαν· μήποτε ἴδωσιν τοῖς ὀφθαλμοῖς καὶ τοῖς ὠσὶν ἀκούσωσιν καὶ τῇ καρδίᾳ συνῶσιν καὶ ἐπιστρέψωσιν, καὶ ἰάσομαι αὐτούς. 16 ὑμῶν δὲ μακάριοι οἱ ὀφθαλμοὶ ὅτι βλέπουσιν, καὶ τὰ ὦτα ὑμῶν ὅτι ἀκούουσιν. 17 ἀμὴν γὰρ λέγω ὑμῖν ὅτι πολλοὶ προφῆται καὶ δίκαιοι ἐπεθύμησαν ἰδεῖν ἃ βλέπετε καὶ οὐκ εἶδαν, καὶ ἀκοῦσαι ἃ ἀκούετε καὶ οὐκ ἤκουσαν

---

[10] And coming near the disciples asked him, "Why do you speak to them in parables?" [11] So answering he said to them, "Because to you it has been given to know the mysteries of the Kingdom of the Heavens, but to them it has not been given. [12] For whoever has, to him it shall be given and he shall be greatly enriched; but whoever does not have, even that which he has shall be taken from him. [13] Because of this I speak in parables to them, because seeing they do not see and hearing they do not hear nor understand; [14] and the prophecy of Isaiah is fulfilled in them saying, 'You will indeed listen and never understand, and indeed see and never perceive.' [15] For the heart of this people has become dull, and those with ears hardly hear, and they closed their eyes; lest they might see with their eyes and hear with their ears and understand with their heart and turn back so that I might heal them. [16] So blessed are your eyes because they see, and your ears because they hear. [17] Amen! For I am saying to you that many prophets and righteous men desired to see what you see and did not see it, and to hear what you hear and did not hear it."

Matthew 13:18-30

18 Ὑμεῖς οὖν ἀκούσατε τὴν παραβολὴν τοῦ σπείραντος. 19 παντὸς ἀκούοντος τὸν λόγον τῆς βασιλείας καὶ μὴ συνιέντος, ἔρχεται ὁ πονηρὸς καὶ ἁρπάζει τὸ ἐσπαρμένον ἐν τῇ καρδίᾳ αὐτοῦ· οὗτός ἐστιν ὁ παρὰ τὴν ὁδὸν σπαρείς. 20 ὁ δὲ ἐπὶ τὰ πετρώδη σπαρείς, οὗτός ἐστιν ὁ τὸν λόγον ἀκούων καὶ εὐθὺς μετὰ χαρᾶς λαμβάνων αὐτόν, 21 οὐκ ἔχει δὲ ῥίζαν ἐν ἑαυτῷ ἀλλὰ πρόσκαιρός ἐστιν, γενομένης δὲ θλίψεως ἢ διωγμοῦ διὰ τὸν λόγον εὐθὺς σκανδαλίζεται. 22 ὁ δὲ εἰς τὰς ἀκάνθας σπαρείς, οὗτός ἐστιν ὁ τὸν λόγον ἀκούων, καὶ ἡ μέριμνα τοῦ αἰῶνος τούτου καὶ ἡ ἀπάτη τοῦ πλούτου συμπνίγει τὸν λόγον, καὶ ἄκαρπος γίνεται. 23 ὁ δὲ ἐπὶ τὴν καλὴν γῆν σπαρείς, οὗτός ἐστιν ὁ τὸν λόγον ἀκούων καὶ συνιείς, ὃς δὴ καρποφορεῖ καὶ ποιεῖ ὃ μὲν ἑκατὸν ὃ δὲ ἑξήκοντα ὃ δὲ τριάκοντα.

24 Ἄλλην παραβολὴν παρέθηκεν αὐτοῖς λέγων·

Ὡμοιώθη ἡ βασιλεία τῶν οὐρανῶν ἀνθρώπῳ σπείραντι καλὸν σπέρμα ἐν τῷ ἀγρῷ αὐτοῦ. 25 ἐν δὲ τῷ καθεύδειν τοὺς ἀνθρώπους ἦλθεν αὐτοῦ ὁ ἐχθρὸς καὶ ἐπέσπειρεν ζιζάνια ἀνὰ μέσον τοῦ σίτου καὶ ἀπῆλθεν. 26 ὅτε δὲ ἐβλάστησεν ὁ χόρτος καὶ καρπὸν ἐποίησεν, τότε ἐφάνη καὶ τὰ ζιζάνια. 27 προσελθόντες δὲ οἱ δοῦλοι τοῦ οἰκοδεσπότου εἶπον αὐτῷ· Κύριε, οὐχὶ καλὸν σπέρμα ἔσπειρας ἐν τῷ σῷ ἀγρῷ; πόθεν οὖν ἔχει ζιζάνια; 28 ὁ δὲ ἔφη αὐτοῖς· Ἐχθρὸς ἄνθρωπος τοῦτο ἐποίησεν. οἱ δὲ δοῦλοι αὐτῷ λέγουσιν· Θέλεις οὖν ἀπελθόντες συλλέξωμεν αὐτά; 29 ὁ δέ φησιν· Οὔ, μήποτε συλλέγοντες τὰ ζιζάνια ἐκριζώσητε ἅμα αὐτοῖς τὸν σῖτον· 30 ἄφετε συναυξάνεσθαι ἀμφότερα μέχρι τοῦ θερισμοῦ· καὶ ἐν καιρῷ τοῦ θερισμοῦ ἐρῶ τοῖς θερισταῖς· Συλλέξατε πρῶτον τὰ ζιζάνια καὶ δήσατε αὐτὰ εἰς δέσμας πρὸς τὸ κατακαῦσαι αὐτά, τὸν δὲ σῖτον συναγάγετε εἰς τὴν ἀποθήκην μου.

18 "Then you yourselves listen to the parable of the sower. 19 When anyone hears the message of the kingdom and does not understand [it], the evil one comes and seizes that which has been sown in his heart; this is what is sown by the road. 20 But that which is sown in rocky places, this is the one who is hearing the word and is immediately receiving it with joy, 21 but he does not have a root in himself so it is transitory, so when trials come or persecution because of the word he immediately falls away. 22 Moreover, that which is sown in the thorns, this is the one hearing the word, yet the anxiety of this age and the deceitfulness of riches chokes the word and it becomes unfruitful. 23 But that which is sown in the good soil, this is the one hearing the word and is understanding, some indeed bear fruit and produces a hundredfold, some sixty, some thirty." 24 Another parable he put before them saying, "The Kingdom of the Heavens is like a man sowing a good seed in his field. 25 But while the people are sleeping his enemy came and sowed tares in the middle of the wheat. 26 Now when the wheat sprouted and produced fruit, then the tares also appeared. 27 So, having come near, the slaves of the householder said to him, 'Master, did you not sow a good seed in your field? From where then does it have tares?' 28 So he answered them, 'A hostile man did this.' But the servants say to him, 'Do you then wish we go gather them?' 29 But he said, 'No, lest you should simultaneously uproot the wheat while gathering the tares with them; 30 permit them both to grow together until the harvest; and at the time of the harvest I shall say to the harvesters, 'Gather first the tares and bind them into a bundle to burn them, now gather the wheat into my storehouse.'"

Matthew 13:31-35

[31] Another parable he put before them saying, "The Kingdom of the Heavens is like a mustard seed, which taking [it] a man sowed in his field; [32] it is the smallest of all seeds, but when it has grown it is larger than the garden plants and becomes a tree, so that the birds of the sky come to nest even in its branches." [33] Another parable he told them, "The Kingdom of the Heavens is like a leaven, which taking [it] a woman hid in three measures of flour until it leavened all of it." [34] All these things Jesus spoke in parables to the crowds, and apart from a parable he was speaking nothing to them; [35] in order that what was spoken by the prophet would be fulfilled saying, "I shall open my mouth in parables, I shall proclaim that which has been hidden from the foundation [of the world]."

Matthew 13:36-50

36 Τότε ἀφεὶς τοὺς ὄχλους ἦλθεν εἰς τὴν οἰκίαν. καὶ προσῆλθον αὐτῷ οἱ μαθηταὶ αὐτοῦ λέγοντες·

Διασάφησον ἡμῖν τὴν παραβολὴν τῶν ζιζανίων τοῦ ἀγροῦ.

37 ὁ δὲ ἀποκριθεὶς εἶπεν·

Ὁ σπείρων τὸ καλὸν σπέρμα ἐστὶν ὁ υἱὸς τοῦ ἀνθρώπου· **38** ὁ δὲ ἀγρός ἐστιν ὁ κόσμος· τὸ δὲ καλὸν σπέρμα, οὗτοί εἰσιν οἱ υἱοὶ τῆς βασιλείας· τὰ δὲ ζιζάνιά εἰσιν οἱ υἱοὶ τοῦ πονηροῦ, **39** ὁ δὲ ἐχθρὸς ὁ σπείρας αὐτά ἐστιν ὁ διάβολος· ὁ δὲ θερισμὸς συντέλεια αἰῶνός ἐστιν, οἱ δὲ θερισταὶ ἄγγελοί εἰσιν. **40** ὥσπερ οὖν συλλέγεται τὰ ζιζάνια καὶ πυρὶ καίεται, οὕτως ἔσται ἐν τῇ συντελείᾳ τοῦ αἰῶνος· **41** ἀποστελεῖ ὁ υἱὸς τοῦ ἀνθρώπου τοὺς ἀγγέλους αὐτοῦ, καὶ συλλέξουσιν ἐκ τῆς βασιλείας αὐτοῦ πάντα τὰ σκάνδαλα καὶ τοὺς ποιοῦντας τὴν ἀνομίαν, **42** καὶ βαλοῦσιν αὐτοὺς εἰς τὴν κάμινον τοῦ πυρός· ἐκεῖ ἔσται ὁ κλαυθμὸς καὶ ὁ βρυγμὸς τῶν ὀδόντων. **43** Τότε οἱ δίκαιοι ἐκλάμψουσιν ὡς ὁ ἥλιος ἐν τῇ βασιλείᾳ τοῦ πατρὸς αὐτῶν. ὁ ἔχων ὦτα ἀκουέτω.

44 Ὁμοία ἐστὶν ἡ βασιλεία τῶν οὐρανῶν θησαυρῷ κεκρυμμένῳ ἐν τῷ ἀγρῷ, ὃν εὑρὼν ἄνθρωπος ἔκρυψεν, καὶ ἀπὸ τῆς χαρᾶς αὐτοῦ ὑπάγει καὶ πωλεῖ πάντα ὅσα ἔχει καὶ ἀγοράζει τὸν ἀγρὸν ἐκεῖνον. **45** Πάλιν ὁμοία ἐστὶν ἡ βασιλεία τῶν οὐρανῶν ἀνθρώπῳ ἐμπόρῳ ζητοῦντι καλοὺς μαργαρίτας· **46** εὑρὼν δὲ ἕνα πολύτιμον μαργαρίτην ἀπελθὼν πέπρακεν πάντα ὅσα εἶχεν καὶ ἠγόρασεν αὐτόν.

47 Πάλιν ὁμοία ἐστὶν ἡ βασιλεία τῶν οὐρανῶν σαγήνῃ βληθείσῃ εἰς τὴν θάλασσαν καὶ ἐκ παντὸς γένους συναγαγούσῃ· **48** ἣν ὅτε ἐπληρώθη ἀναβιβάσαντες ἐπὶ τὸν αἰγιαλὸν καὶ καθίσαντες συνέλεξαν τὰ καλὰ εἰς ἄγγη, τὰ δὲ σαπρὰ ἔξω ἔβαλον. **49** οὕτως ἔσται ἐν τῇ συντελείᾳ τοῦ αἰῶνος· ἐξελεύσονται οἱ ἄγγελοι καὶ ἀφοριοῦσιν τοὺς πονηροὺς ἐκ μέσου τῶν δικαίων **50** καὶ βαλοῦσιν αὐτοὺς εἰς τὴν κάμινον τοῦ πυρός· ἐκεῖ ἔσται ὁ κλαυθμὸς καὶ ὁ βρυγμὸς τῶν ὀδόντων.

36 Then having dismissed the crowds he entered into the house. And his disciples came to him saying, "Explain to us the parables of the tares of the field." **37** So answering he said, "He who sows the good seed is the Son of Man; **38** and the field is the world; now the good seed, these are the sons of the kingdom; but the tares are the sons of the evil one, **39** and the hostile one who sowed them is the devil; and the harvest is the end of the age, and the harvesters are angels. **40** Then just as the tares are gathered and burned up with fire, so it shall be at the end of the age; the **41** Son of Man shall send his angels, and they shall gather from his kingdom all the stumbling-blocks and those practicing lawlessness, **42** and throw them into the fiery furnace; in that place there shall be weeping and gnashing of the teeth. **43** Then the righteous shall shine like the sun in the kingdom of their Father. The one who has ears, Listen! **44** The Kingdom of the Heavens is like a treasure hidden in the field, which finding [it] a man hid, and out of his joy he leaves and sells everything, as much as he has, and buys that field. **45** Again, the Kingdom of the Heavens is like a merchant seeking beautiful pearls; **46** so having found one precious pearl, departing, he sold everything that he had and bought it. **47** Again, the Kingdom of the Heavens is like a fishing net that was being cast into the sea and caught every kind [of fish]; **48** which when it was filled, having brought it up to the shore and, sitting down, they gathered the good into containers, but the worthless they threw out. **49** Thus it shall be at the end of the age; the angels shall go out and separate the evil from the midst of the righteous **50** and throw them into the fiery furnace; in that place there shall be weeping and gnashing of teeth."

Matthew 13:51-58

Matthew 14:1-12

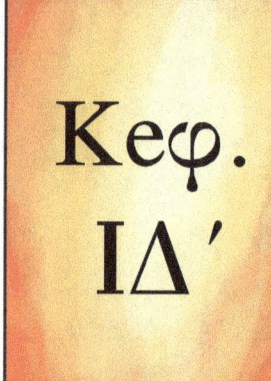

14:1 At that time Herod the Tetrarch heard of the fame of Jesus, 2 and he said to his servants, "This is John the Baptist; he was raised from the dead, and because of this the powerful deeds are at work in him. 3 For Herod, arresting John, bound him and put him in prison because of Herodias, the wife of Phillip his brother, 4 for John was saying to him, "It is not right for you to have her;" 5 and [although] wanting to kill him he feared the crowd, because they were holding him as a prophet. 6 Now when Herod's birthday took place the daughter of Herodias danced in the midst and it pleased Herod, 7 wherefore he promised with an oath to give her whatever she might ask. 8 So after being prompted by her mother, "Give me," she says, "here on a platter the head of John the Baptist." 9 And having grieved, the king, because of the oaths and those reclining [with him], commanded [it] to be given, 10 and sending forth [emissaries] he beheaded John in the prison; 11 and his head was brought on a platter and given to the girl, and she brought it to her mother. 12 And coming his disciples took away the corpse and buried it, and going they reported [it] to Jesus.

Matthew 14:13-21

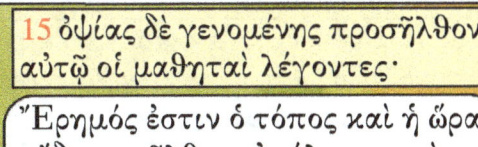

13 Ἀκούσας δὲ ὁ Ἰησοῦς ἀνεχώρησεν ἐκεῖθεν ἐν πλοίῳ εἰς ἔρημον τόπον κατ' ἰδίαν· καὶ ἀκούσαντες οἱ ὄχλοι ἠκολούθησαν αὐτῷ πεζῇ ἀπὸ τῶν πόλεων. 14 καὶ ἐξελθὼν εἶδεν πολὺν ὄχλον, καὶ ἐσπλαγχνίσθη ἐπ' αὐτοῖς καὶ ἐθεράπευσεν τοὺς ἀρρώστους αὐτῶν.

15 ὀψίας δὲ γενομένης προσῆλθον αὐτῷ οἱ μαθηταὶ λέγοντες·

Ἔρημός ἐστιν ὁ τόπος καὶ ἡ ὥρα ἤδη παρῆλθεν· ἀπόλυσον τοὺς ὄχλους, ἵνα ἀπελθόντες εἰς τὰς κώμας ἀγοράσωσιν ἑαυτοῖς βρώματα.

16 ὁ δὲ Ἰησοῦς εἶπεν αὐτοῖς·

Οὐ χρείαν ἔχουσιν ἀπελθεῖν· δότε αὐτοῖς ὑμεῖς φαγεῖν.

17 οἱ δὲ λέγουσιν αὐτῷ·

Οὐκ ἔχομεν ὧδε εἰ μὴ πέντε ἄρτους καὶ δύο ἰχθύας.

18 ὁ δὲ εἶπεν·

Φέρετέ μοι ὧδε αὐτούς.

19 καὶ κελεύσας τοὺς ὄχλους ἀνακλιθῆναι ἐπὶ τοῦ χόρτου, λαβὼν τοὺς πέντε ἄρτους καὶ τοὺς δύο ἰχθύας, ἀναβλέψας εἰς τὸν οὐρανὸν εὐλόγησεν καὶ κλάσας ἔδωκεν τοῖς μαθηταῖς τοὺς ἄρτους οἱ δὲ μαθηταὶ τοῖς ὄχλοις. 20 καὶ ἔφαγον πάντες καὶ ἐχορτάσθησαν, καὶ ἦραν τὸ περισσεῦον τῶν κλασμάτων δώδεκα κοφίνους πλήρεις. 21 οἱ δὲ ἐσθίοντες ἦσαν ἄνδρες ὡσεὶ πεντακισχίλιοι χωρὶς γυναικῶν καὶ παιδίων.

[13] So, hearing [this] Jesus withdrew from there in a boat to a deserted place by himself; and when the crowds heard they followed him on foot from the towns. [14] And coming out he saw a great crowd and he had compassion on them and healed their sick. [15] But when evening came the disciples came to him saying, "This is a deserted place and the hour is already late; release the crowds, so that, departing into the villages, they might buy themselves food." [16] But Jesus said to them, "They do not need to go away; you give them [something] to eat." [17] But they said to him, "We have nothing here except five loaves of bread and two fish!" [18] So he said, "Bring them here to me." [19] And ordering the crowds to lay down on the grass, taking the five loaves and two fish, looking up to heaven he blessed [them] and breaking [them] he gave the disciples the loaves and the disciples to the crowds. [20] And everyone ate and were satisfied, and they took away 12 full baskets of that which was left of the broken pieces. [21] Now those eating were about 5000 men aside from women and children.

Matthew 14:22-31

[22] And immediately he compelled the disciples to embark onto a boat and to go before him to the other side, while he released the crowds. [23] And having released the crowds he ascended the mountain by himself to pray. So when evening came he was there alone. [24] But the boat was already many stadia away from the land, being battered by the waves, for the wind was against [it]. [25] But in the fourth watch of the night he came towards them walking upon the sea. [26] So when the disciples saw him walking upon the sea they were troubled saying, "It is a ghost!" and they cried out in fear. [27] But immediately Jesus spoke to them saying, "Be of good courage, it is I; do not be afraid." [28] Now answering back to him Peter said, "Lord, if it is you, call me to come to you on the water;" [29] so he said, "Come." And descending from the boat Peter walked upon the water and came towards Jesus. [30] But seeing the strong wind he was afraid, and beginning to sink he cried out saying, "Lord, save me." [31] So immediately Jesus, stretching out the hand, took hold of him and says to him, "You of little faith, why did you doubt"?

Matthew 14:32-15:9

32 καὶ ἀναβάντων αὐτῶν εἰς τὸ πλοῖον ἐκόπασεν ὁ ἄνεμος. 33 οἱ δὲ ἐν τῷ πλοίῳ προσεκύνησαν αὐτῷ λέγοντες·

Ἀληθῶς θεοῦ υἱὸς εἶ.

34 Καὶ διαπεράσαντες ἦλθον ἐπὶ τὴν γῆν εἰς Γεννησαρέτ. 35 καὶ ἐπιγνόντες αὐτὸν οἱ ἄνδρες τοῦ τόπου ἐκείνου ἀπέστειλαν εἰς ὅλην τὴν περίχωρον ἐκείνην, καὶ προσήνεγκαν αὐτῷ πάντας τοὺς κακῶς ἔχοντας, 36 καὶ παρεκάλουν αὐτὸν ἵνα μόνον ἅψωνται τοῦ κρασπέδου τοῦ ἱματίου αὐτοῦ· καὶ ὅσοι ἥψαντο διεσώθησαν.

Κεφ. ΙΕ΄

15:1 Τότε προσέρχονται τῷ Ἰησοῦ ἀπὸ Ἱεροσολύμων Φαρισαῖοι καὶ γραμματεῖς λέγοντες·

2 Διὰ τί οἱ μαθηταί σου παραβαίνουσιν τὴν παράδοσιν τῶν πρεσβυτέρων; οὐ γὰρ νίπτονται τὰς χεῖρας αὐτῶν ὅταν ἄρτον ἐσθίωσιν.

3 ὁ δὲ ἀποκριθεὶς εἶπεν αὐτοῖς·

Διὰ τί καὶ ὑμεῖς παραβαίνετε τὴν ἐντολὴν τοῦ θεοῦ διὰ τὴν παράδοσιν ὑμῶν; 4 ὁ γὰρ θεὸς εἶπεν· Τίμα τὸν πατέρα καὶ τὴν μητέρα, καί· Ὁ κακολογῶν πατέρα ἢ μητέρα θανάτῳ τελευτάτω· 5 ὑμεῖς δὲ λέγετε· Ὃς ἂν εἴπῃ τῷ πατρὶ ἢ τῇ μητρί· Δῶρον ὃ ἐὰν ἐξ ἐμοῦ ὠφεληθῇς, 6 οὐ μὴ τιμήσει τὸν πατέρα αὐτοῦ· καὶ ἠκυρώσατε τὸν λόγον τοῦ θεοῦ διὰ τὴν παράδοσιν ὑμῶν. 7 ὑποκριταί, καλῶς ἐπροφήτευσεν περὶ ὑμῶν Ἠσαΐας λέγων·

8 Ὁ λαὸς οὗτος τοῖς χείλεσίν με τιμᾷ, ἡ δὲ καρδία αὐτῶν πόρρω ἀπέχει ἀπ' ἐμοῦ· 9 μάτην δὲ σέβονταί με, διδάσκοντες διδασκαλίας ἐντάλματα ἀνθρώπων.

32 And when they had gotten into the boat the wind ceased. 33 Now those in the boat bowed down to him saying, "Truly you are the Son of God." 34 And crossing over they came to the land at Gennesaret. 35 And having recognized him the men of that place sent [word] to the entirety of that surrounding region and they brought to him all who had an illness, 36 and they were calling out to him that they might only touch the fringe of his garment; and as many who touched him were cured. 15:1 Then Pharisees and Scribes from Jerusalem come to Jesus saying, 2 "Why do your disciples transgress the tradition of the elders? For they do not wash their hands when they eat bread." 3 So answering back he said to them, "Why do you also transgress the command of God for the sake of your tradition? 4 For God said, 'Honor your father and mother,' and 'The one who speaks evil of father or mother shall surely die;' 5 but you yourselves say, 'Whoever says to father or mother; If something should have benefitted you from me [it is now] a temple gift,' 6 he shall certainly not honor his father; and you revoked the word of God by your tradition. 7 Hypocrites! Isaiah prophesied well about you saying, 8 'This people honor me with their lips but their hearts are far from me; 9 so they worship me in vain, teaching as doctrine the commandments of people.'"

Matthew 15:10-21

[10] And summoning the crowd he said to them, "Listen and understand; [11] that which enters into the mouth does not defile the person, but that which comes out of the mouth this defiles the person." [12] Then, coming near, the disciples say to him, "Do you know that the Pharisees, hearing the word, were offended?" [13] So answering back he said, "Every plant that my heavenly Father did not plant shall be uprooted. [14] Let them be; they are blind guides of the blind; now if a blind person guides a blind person, both shall fall into a pit." [15] But answering back Peter said to him, "Explain to us this parable." [16] So he said, "Are you even still without understanding? [17] Do you understand that anything that enters into the mouth passes into the belly and is expelled into a latrine? [Surely, yes!] [18] But that which comes out of the mouth comes from the heart, and those things defile the person. [19] For out of the heart come evil thoughts, murders, adulteries, fornications, thefts, false testimonies, blasphemies. [20] These are the things that defile the person, but to eat with unwashed hands does not defile the person." [21] And having left from there Jesus withdrew into the region of Tyre and Sidon.

Matthew 15:22-30

[22] And behold a Canaanite woman from those regions, coming out, kept crying out saying, "Have mercy on me, Lord, Son of David; my daughter is badly demon possessed." [23] But he did not answer her a word. And having approached, his disciples were asking him saying, "Get rid of her, because she keeps crying out behind us." [24] So answering [her] back he said, "I was not sent except to the lost sheep of the house of Israel." [25] But she, having come, was bowing down to him saying, "Lord, help me!" [26] But answering back he said, "It is not good to take the bread of the children and throw it to the dogs." [27] But she said, "Yes, Lord, for even the dogs eat from the scraps that are falling from the table of their masters." [28] Then answering back Jesus said to her, "O woman, great [is] your faith; let it be to you as you will." And her daughter was healed at that hour. [29] And having departed from there Jesus went alongside the sea of Galilee, and ascending the mountain he was sitting there. [30] And great crowds came to him having with them mute, blind, lame, crippled and many others, and they laid them at this feet, and he healed them;

Matthew 15:31-38

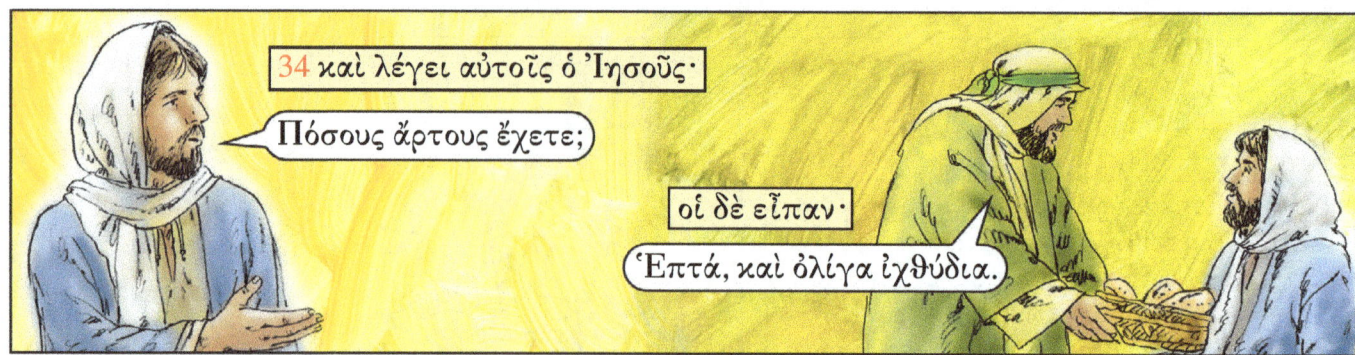

[31] so the crowd marveled seeing the mute speaking the crippled healthy and the lame walking and the blind seeing; and they glorified the God of Israel. [32] Now Jesus, summoning his disciples, said, "I have compassion on the crowd, because they have already remained with me for three days and they do not have something they might eat; and I do not wish to send them away hungry, lest they might faint on the way." [33] And the disciples say to him, "Where, in a wilderness so great, [can] we [get] bread as to satisfy such a great crowd?" [34] And Jesus says to them, "How much bread do you have?" So they said, "Seven [loaves of bread] and a few fish." [35] And commanding the crowd to recline on the ground [36] he took the seven [loaves of] bread and the fish and giving thanks he broke [the bread] and was giving it to the disciples and the disciples to the crowds. [37] And everyone ate and were satisfied, and they took away seven large full baskets of that which was left over from the broken bread. [38] Now those eating were 4000 men apart from women and children.

Matthew 15:39-16:11

39 καὶ ἀπολύσας τοὺς ὄχλους ἐνέβη εἰς τὸ πλοῖον, καὶ ἦλθεν εἰς τὰ ὅρια Μαγαδάν.

Κεφ. IϚ΄

16:1 Καὶ προσελθόντες οἱ Φαρισαῖοι καὶ Σαδδουκαῖοι πειράζοντες ἐπηρώτησαν αὐτὸν σημεῖον ἐκ τοῦ οὐρανοῦ ἐπιδεῖξαι αὐτοῖς. 2 ὁ δὲ ἀποκριθεὶς εἶπεν αὐτοῖς·

Ὀψίας γενομένης λέγετε· Εὐδία, πυρράζει γὰρ ὁ οὐρανός· 3 καὶ πρωΐ· Σήμερον χειμών, πυρράζει γὰρ στυγνάζων ὁ οὐρανός.

τὸ μὲν πρόσωπον τοῦ οὐρανοῦ γινώσκετε διακρίνειν, τὰ δὲ σημεῖα τῶν καιρῶν οὐ δύνασθε. 4 Γενεὰ πονηρὰ καὶ μοιχαλὶς σημεῖον ἐπιζητεῖ, καὶ σημεῖον οὐ δοθήσεται αὐτῇ εἰ μὴ τὸ σημεῖον Ἰωνᾶ.

καὶ καταλιπὼν αὐτοὺς ἀπῆλθεν. 5 Καὶ ἐλθόντες οἱ μαθηταὶ εἰς τὸ πέραν ἐπελάθοντο ἄρτους λαβεῖν. 6 ὁ δὲ Ἰησοῦς εἶπεν αὐτοῖς·

Ὁρᾶτε καὶ προσέχετε ἀπὸ τῆς ζύμης τῶν Φαρισαίων καὶ Σαδδουκαίων.

7 οἱ δὲ διελογίζοντο ἐν ἑαυτοῖς λέγοντες ὅτι

Ἄρτους οὐκ ἐλάβομεν.

8 γνοὺς δὲ ὁ Ἰησοῦς εἶπεν·

Τί διαλογίζεσθε ἐν ἑαυτοῖς, ὀλιγόπιστοι, ὅτι ἄρτους οὐκ ἐλάβετε; 9 οὔπω νοεῖτε, οὐδὲ μνημονεύετε τοὺς πέντε ἄρτους τῶν πεντακισχιλίων καὶ πόσους κοφίνους ἐλάβετε; 10 οὐδὲ τοὺς ἑπτὰ ἄρτους τῶν τετρακισχιλίων καὶ πόσας σπυρίδας ἐλάβετε; 11 πῶς οὐ νοεῖτε ὅτι οὐ περὶ ἄρτων εἶπον ὑμῖν; προσέχετε δὲ ἀπὸ τῆς ζύμης τῶν Φαρισαίων καὶ Σαδδουκαίων.

[39] And dismissing the crowds he embarked onto the boat, and he came to the borders of Magadan. [16:1] And coming forward the Pharisees and Sadducees, testing [Jesus], asked him to show them a sign from heaven. [2] But answering back he said to them, "When evening comes you say; 'fair weather, for the sky [is] red'; [3] and in the morning; 'bad weather today, for the sky is red, threatening.' You know how to discern the appearance of the sky, but the signs of the times you are unable. [4] Evil and adulterous generation which seeks for a sign, and a sign shall not be given to it except the sign of Jonah." And leaving them he went away. [5] And having come to the other side, the disciples forgot to take bread. [6] So Jesus said to them, "Watch out and take heed of the leaven of the Pharisees and the Sadducees." [7] Now they were debating amongst themselves saying this, "We did not take any bread." [8] But knowing [this] Jesus said, "Why are you debating amongst yourselves, you of little faith, that you did not bring bread; [9] do you not yet understand, nor remember the five loaves of bread of the 5000 and how many baskets you took? [Surely, yes!] [10] Nor the seven loaves of bread of the 4000 and how many baskets you took? [Surely, yes!] [11] How do you not understand that I did not speak to you about bread? But take heed of the leaven of the Pharisees and Sadducees."

Matthew 16:12-20

[12] Then they understood that he did not say to take heed of the leaven of the loaves of bread but of the teaching of the Pharisees and Sadducees. [13] Now Jesus, having come into the district of Caesarea Philippi, was asking his disciples saying, "Who do people say the Son of Man is?" [14] So they said, "Some they [say] John the Baptist, now others Elijah, additionally others Jeremiah or one of the prophets." [15] He says to them, "But who do you say that I am?" [16] So answering back Simon Peter said, "You are the Christ the Son of the living God." [17] So answering back Jesus said to him, "Blessed are you, Simon bar-Jonah, for flesh and blood did not reveal [it] to you but my Father who [is] in the heavens; [18] so I myself also say to you this: 'You yourself are Peter, and upon this rock I shall build my assembly, and gates of Hades shall not prevail against it; [19] I shall give you the keys of the Kingdom of the Heavens, and whatever you bind on the earth shall be bound in the heavens, and whatever you loose on the earth shall be loosed in the heavens.'" [20] Then he charged the disciples that none of them may say that he is the Messiah.

Matthew 16:21-17:1

21 Ἀπὸ τότε ἤρξατο ὁ Ἰησοῦς δεικνύειν τοῖς μαθηταῖς αὐτοῦ ὅτι δεῖ αὐτὸν εἰς Ἱεροσόλυμα ἀπελθεῖν καὶ πολλὰ παθεῖν ἀπὸ τῶν πρεσβυτέρων καὶ ἀρχιερέων καὶ γραμματέων καὶ ἀποκτανθῆναι καὶ τῇ τρίτῃ ἡμέρᾳ ἐγερθῆναι. **22** καὶ προσλαβόμενος αὐτὸν ὁ Πέτρος ἤρξατο ἐπιτιμᾶν αὐτῷ λέγων·

"Ἵλεώς σοι, κύριε· οὐ μὴ ἔσται σοι τοῦτο.

23 ὁ δὲ στραφεὶς εἶπεν τῷ Πέτρῳ·

"Ὕπαγε ὀπίσω μου, Σατανᾶ· σκάνδαλον εἶ ἐμοῦ, ὅτι οὐ φρονεῖς τὰ τοῦ θεοῦ ἀλλὰ τὰ τῶν ἀνθρώπων.

24 Τότε ὁ Ἰησοῦς εἶπεν τοῖς μαθηταῖς αὐτοῦ·

Εἴ τις θέλει ὀπίσω μου ἐλθεῖν, ἀπαρνησάσθω ἑαυτὸν καὶ ἀράτω τὸν σταυρὸν αὐτοῦ καὶ ἀκολουθείτω μοι. **25** ὃς γὰρ ἐὰν θέλῃ τὴν ψυχὴν αὐτοῦ σῶσαι ἀπολέσει αὐτήν· ὃς δ' ἂν ἀπολέσῃ τὴν ψυχὴν αὐτοῦ ἕνεκεν ἐμοῦ εὑρήσει αὐτήν. **26** τί γὰρ ὠφεληθήσεται ἄνθρωπος ἐὰν τὸν κόσμον ὅλον κερδήσῃ τὴν δὲ ψυχὴν αὐτοῦ ζημιωθῇ; ἢ τί δώσει ἄνθρωπος ἀντάλλαγμα τῆς ψυχῆς αὐτοῦ;

27 μέλλει γὰρ ὁ υἱὸς τοῦ ἀνθρώπου ἔρχεσθαι ἐν τῇ δόξῃ τοῦ πατρὸς αὐτοῦ μετὰ τῶν ἀγγέλων αὐτοῦ, καὶ τότε ἀποδώσει ἑκάστῳ κατὰ τὴν πρᾶξιν αὐτοῦ. **28** ἀμὴν λέγω ὑμῖν ὅτι εἰσίν τινες τῶν ὧδε ἑστώτων οἵτινες οὐ μὴ γεύσωνται θανάτου ἕως ἂν ἴδωσιν τὸν υἱὸν τοῦ ἀνθρώπου ἐρχόμενον ἐν τῇ βασιλείᾳ αὐτοῦ.

17:1 Καὶ μεθ' ἡμέρας ἓξ παραλαμβάνει ὁ Ἰησοῦς τὸν Πέτρον καὶ Ἰάκωβον καὶ Ἰωάννην τὸν ἀδελφὸν αὐτοῦ, καὶ ἀναφέρει αὐτοὺς εἰς ὄρος ὑψηλὸν κατ' ἰδίαν.

Κεφ. ΙΖ΄

21 From then on Jesus began to show his disciples that it was necessary for him to go to Jerusalem and to suffer much from the elders and chief priests and scribes and to be killed and on the third day be raised. **22** And taking him aside Peter began to rebuke him saying, "[God be] merciful to you, Lord; this shall certainly not happen to you." **23** But turning around he said to Peter, "Get behind me, Satan! You are a stumbling block to me, for you do not think of the things of God but of the things of humans." **24** Then Jesus said to his disciples, "If someone wishes to come after me, he must deny himself and take up his cross and follow me. **25** For whoever wishes to save his life he shall lose it; but whoever loses his life on account of me he shall find it. **26** For what shall a person profit if he were to gain the whole world but his life be forfeited? Or what shall a person give in exchange for his life? **27** For the Son of Man is about to come in the glory of his Father with his angels, and then he shall give to each according to his deeds. **28** Amen! I am saying to you this: 'There are some standing here who shall certainly not taste death until they behold the Son of Man coming in his kingdom.'" **17:1** And after six days Jesus takes Peter and James and John his brother, and leads them up a high mountain by themselves.

Matthew 17:2-10

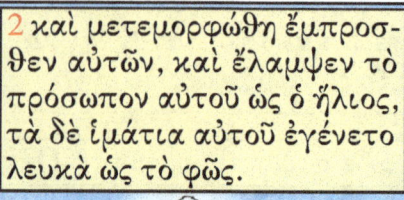

[2] And he was transformed before them, and his face shone like the sun, moreover his garments became white as light. [3] And behold Moses and Elijah appeared to them speaking with him. [4] Now answering back Peter said to Jesus, "Lord, it is good for us to be here; if you wish, I shall make here three dwellings, one for you and one for Moses and one for Elijah." [5] While he was still speaking behold a bright cloud overshadowed them, and behold a voice out of the cloud saying, "This is my beloved son, in whom I am well-pleased; listen to him." [6] And hearing [this] the disciples fell on their faces and were exceedingly afraid. [7] And Jesus came forward and touching them said, "Arise and do not be afraid." [8] Now having lifted up their eyes they saw no one except Jesus alone. [9] And as they are descending from the mountain Jesus commanded them saying, "Tell no one of the vision until the Son of Man is raised from the dead." [10] And his disciples asked him saying, "Why then do the scribes say that it is necessary for Elijah to come first?"

Matthew 17:11-20

[11] So answering he said, "Elijah is coming and shall restore everything; [12] but I am saying to you that Elijah already came, and they did not recognize him but they did to him whatever they liked; thus also the Son of Man is about to suffer by them." [13] Then the disciples understood that he spoke to them about John the Baptist. [14] And when they came toward the crowd a person approached him falling on his knees [15] and saying, "Lord, have mercy on my son, for he has seizures and suffers badly, for often he falls into the fire and often into the water. [16] And I brought him to your disciples, and they did not have the power to heal him." [17] So answering back Jesus said, "O faithless and perverse generation, how long shall I be with you? How long shall I endure you? Bring him here to me!" [18] And Jesus rebuked him, and the demon came out of him; and the boy was healed from that hour. [19] Then the disciples having come to Jesus privately said, "Why were we not able to cast it out?" [20] So he says to them,

Matthew 17:20-27

Κεφ. ΙΗ´

"Because of your little faith; for Amen! I am saying to you, if you have faith as a mustard seed, you shall say to this mountain, 'Go from here to there,' and it shall go, and nothing shall be impossible to you." [22] Now having gathered together in the Galilee Jesus said to them, "The Son of Man is about to be handed over into the hands of people, [23] and they shall kill him, and on the third day he shall be raised." And they were deeply grieved. [24] Now having come to Capernaum the two-drachmae collectors approached Peter and said, "Does your teacher pay the two-drachmae [tax]?" [Surely, yes!] [25] He says, "Yes." And coming into the house Jesus anticipated him saying, "What do you think, Simon? The kings of the earth, from whom do they receive tax or poll-tax? From their sons or others?" [26] So when he said, "From others," Jesus said to him, "Then the sons really are exempt! [27] But in order that we not cause them to stumble, go to the sea to cast a fishhook and take away the first fish that comes up, and opening its mouth you shall find a stater; take that to give them for me and you."

Matthew 18:1-14

18:1 Ἐν ἐκείνῃ τῇ ὥρᾳ προσῆλθον οἱ μαθηταὶ τῷ Ἰησοῦ λέγοντες·

Τίς ἄρα μείζων ἐστὶν ἐν τῇ βασιλείᾳ τῶν οὐρανῶν;

2 καὶ προσκαλεσάμενος παιδίον ἔστησεν αὐτὸ ἐν μέσῳ αὐτῶν **3** καὶ εἶπεν·

Ἀμὴν λέγω ὑμῖν, ἐὰν μὴ στραφῆτε καὶ γένησθε ὡς τὰ παιδία, οὐ μὴ εἰσέλθητε εἰς τὴν βασιλείαν τῶν οὐρανῶν. **4** ὅστις οὖν ταπεινώσει ἑαυτὸν ὡς τὸ παιδίον τοῦτο, οὗτός ἐστιν ὁ μείζων ἐν τῇ βασιλείᾳ τῶν οὐρανῶν· **5** καὶ ὃς ἐὰν δέξηται ἓν παιδίον τοιοῦτο ἐπὶ τῷ ὀνόματί μου, ἐμὲ δέχεται.

6 Ὃς δ' ἂν σκανδαλίσῃ ἕνα τῶν μικρῶν τούτων τῶν πιστευόντων εἰς ἐμέ, συμφέρει αὐτῷ ἵνα κρεμασθῇ μύλος ὀνικὸς εἰς τὸν τράχηλον αὐτοῦ καὶ καταποντισθῇ ἐν τῷ πελάγει τῆς θαλάσσης. **7** οὐαὶ τῷ κόσμῳ ἀπὸ τῶν σκανδάλων· ἀνάγκη γὰρ ἐλθεῖν τὰ σκάνδαλα, πλὴν οὐαὶ τῷ ἀνθρώπῳ δι' οὗ τὸ σκάνδαλον ἔρχεται. **8** Εἰ δὲ ἡ χείρ σου ἢ ὁ πούς σου σκανδαλίζει σε, ἔκκοψον αὐτὸν καὶ βάλε ἀπὸ σοῦ· καλόν σοί ἐστιν εἰσελθεῖν εἰς τὴν ζωὴν κυλλὸν ἢ χωλόν, ἢ δύο χεῖρας ἢ δύο πόδας ἔχοντα βληθῆναι εἰς τὸ πῦρ τὸ αἰώνιον. **9** καὶ εἰ ὁ ὀφθαλμός σου σκανδαλίζει σε, ἔξελε αὐτὸν καὶ βάλε ἀπὸ σοῦ· καλόν σοί ἐστιν μονόφθαλμον εἰς τὴν ζωὴν εἰσελθεῖν, ἢ δύο ὀφθαλμοὺς ἔχοντα βληθῆναι εἰς τὴν γέενναν τοῦ πυρός.

10 Ὁρᾶτε μὴ καταφρονήσητε ἑνὸς τῶν μικρῶν τούτων, λέγω γὰρ ὑμῖν ὅτι οἱ ἄγγελοι αὐτῶν ἐν οὐρανοῖς διὰ παντὸς βλέπουσι τὸ πρόσωπον τοῦ πατρός μου τοῦ ἐν οὐρανοῖς. **12** τί ὑμῖν δοκεῖ; ἐὰν γένηταί τινι ἀνθρώπῳ ἑκατὸν πρόβατα καὶ πλανηθῇ ἓν ἐξ αὐτῶν, οὐχὶ ἀφήσει τὰ ἐνενήκοντα ἐννέα ἐπὶ τὰ ὄρη καὶ πορευθεὶς ζητεῖ τὸ πλανώμενον; **13** καὶ ἐὰν γένηται εὑρεῖν αὐτό, ἀμὴν λέγω ὑμῖν ὅτι χαίρει ἐπ' αὐτῷ μᾶλλον ἢ ἐπὶ τοῖς ἐνενήκοντα ἐννέα τοῖς μὴ πεπλανημένοις. **14** οὕτως οὐκ ἔστιν θέλημα ἔμπροσθεν τοῦ πατρὸς ὑμῶν τοῦ ἐν οὐρανοῖς ἵνα ἀπόληται ἓν τῶν μικρῶν τούτων.

18:1 At that hour the disciples came to Jesus saying, "Who, then, is [the] greatest in the Kingdom of the Heavens?" **2** And calling over a child he placed him in their midst **3** and said, "Amen! I am saying to you, unless you be changed and become like children, you will certainly not enter into the Kingdom of the Heavens. **4** So then whoever shall humble himself like this child, he is the greatest in the Kingdom of the Heavens; **5** and he who might welcome one such child in my name, welcomes me. **6** But whoever might cause one of the least of these who believe in me to stumble, it would be better for him that a great millstone be hung around his neck and that he be drowned in the depths of the sea. **7** Woe to the world for its stumbling blocks! For it is inevitable for stumbling blocks to come, but woe to the person through whom the stumbling block comes! **8** So, if your hand or your foot causes you to stumble, cut it off and throw it away from you; it is better for you to enter into life maimed or lame, than, having two hands or two feet, to be thrown into the eternal fire. **9** And if your eye causes you to stumble, tear it out and throw it away from you; it is better for you to enter into life being one-eyed, than, having two eyes, to be thrown into the Gehenna of Fire. **10** See to it that you do not despise one of these little ones, for I am telling you that their angels in the heavens always see the face of my Father who is in the heavens. **12** What do you think? If a certain person has 100 sheep and one of them wanders away, will he not leave the 99 on the mountain and, going, seek the one that is lost? **13** And if he happens to find it, Amen! I am saying to you that he rejoices more over it than over the 99 who were not lost. **14** So it is not the will before your Father who is in the heavens that one of these little ones should perish."

Matthew 18:15-25

15 Ἐὰν δὲ ἁμαρτήσῃ εἰς σὲ ὁ ἀδελφός σου, ὕπαγε ἔλεγξον αὐτὸν μεταξὺ σοῦ καὶ αὐτοῦ μόνου. ἐὰν σου ἀκούσῃ, ἐκέρδησας τὸν ἀδελφόν σου· 16 ἐὰν δὲ μὴ ἀκούσῃ, παράλαβε μετὰ σοῦ ἔτι ἕνα ἢ δύο, ἵνα ἐπὶ στόματος δύο μαρτύρων ἢ τριῶν σταθῇ πᾶν ῥῆμα· 17 ἐὰν δὲ παρακούσῃ αὐτῶν, εἰπὸν τῇ ἐκκλησίᾳ· ἐὰν δὲ καὶ τῆς ἐκκλησίας παρακούσῃ, ἔστω σοι ὥσπερ ὁ ἐθνικὸς καὶ ὁ τελώνης. 18 ἀμὴν λέγω ὑμῖν, ὅσα ἐὰν δήσητε ἐπὶ τῆς γῆς ἔσται δεδεμένα ἐν οὐρανῷ καὶ ὅσα ἐὰν λύσητε ἐπὶ τῆς γῆς ἔσται λελυμένα ἐν οὐρανῷ. 19 Πάλιν ἀμὴν λέγω ὑμῖν ὅτι ἐὰν δύο συμφωνήσωσιν ἐξ ὑμῶν ἐπὶ τῆς γῆς περὶ παντὸς πράγματος οὗ ἐὰν αἰτήσωνται, γενήσεται αὐτοῖς παρὰ τοῦ πατρός μου τοῦ ἐν οὐρανοῖς.

20 οὗ γάρ εἰσιν δύο ἢ τρεῖς συνηγμένοι εἰς τὸ ἐμὸν ὄνομα, ἐκεῖ εἰμι ἐν μέσῳ αὐτῶν.

21 Τότε προσελθὼν αὐτῷ ὁ Πέτρος εἶπεν·

Κύριε, ποσάκις ἁμαρτήσει εἰς ἐμὲ ὁ ἀδελφός μου καὶ ἀφήσω αὐτῷ; ἕως ἑπτάκις;

22 λέγει αὐτῷ ὁ Ἰησοῦς·

Οὐ λέγω σοι ἕως ἑπτάκις ἀλλὰ ἕως ἑβδομηκοντάκις ἑπτά. 23 Διὰ τοῦτο ὡμοιώθη ἡ βασιλεία τῶν οὐρανῶν ἀνθρώπῳ βασιλεῖ ὃς ἠθέλησεν συνᾶραι λόγον μετὰ τῶν δούλων αὐτοῦ· 24 ἀρξαμένου δὲ αὐτοῦ συναίρειν προσηνέχθη αὐτῷ εἷς ὀφειλέτης μυρίων ταλάντων. 25 μὴ ἔχοντος δὲ αὐτοῦ ἀποδοῦναι ἐκέλευσεν αὐτὸν ὁ κύριος πραθῆναι καὶ τὴν γυναῖκα καὶ τὰ τέκνα καὶ πάντα ὅσα ἔχει καὶ ἀποδοθῆναι.

[15] "So, if your brother sins against you, go, reprove him between you and him alone. If he listens to you, you have won over your brother; [16] but if he does not listen, bring with you even one or two, so that on the basis of two or three witnesses every word might be established. [17] But if he refuses to listen to them, tell the assembly; now if he even refuses to listen to the assembly, let him be as a Gentile and a tax collector. [18] Amen! I am saying to you, whatever you bind on earth shall be bound in heaven and whatever you loose on earth shall be loosed in heaven. [19] Again, Amen! I am saying to you that if two of you agree on the earth about anything they might ask, it shall be done to them by my Father who is in the heavens. [20] For where two or three are gathered in my name, there I am in their midst." [21] Then approaching him Peter said, "Lord, how often shall my brother sin against me and I shall forgive him? Until seven times?" [22] Jesus says to him, "I do not say to you until seven times but until seventy-seven times. [23] Because of this the Kingdom of the Heavens is like a man, a king, who wished to settle accounts with his slaves; [24] so when he began to settle accounts a debtor of ten thousand talents was brought to him. [25] But since he has nothing with which to pay back [the debt] the lord ordered him to be sold, also the wife and the children and everything he has, and to be paid back."

Matthew 18:26-19:2

26 πεσὼν οὖν ὁ δοῦλος προσεκύνει αὐτῷ λέγων· Μακροθύμησον ἐπ' ἐμοί, καὶ πάντα ἀποδώσω σοι. 27 σπλαγχνισθεὶς δὲ ὁ κύριος τοῦ δούλου ἐκείνου ἀπέλυσεν αὐτόν, καὶ τὸ δάνειον ἀφῆκεν αὐτῷ. 28 ἐξελθὼν δὲ ὁ δοῦλος ἐκεῖνος εὗρεν ἕνα τῶν συνδούλων αὐτοῦ ὃς ὤφειλεν αὐτῷ ἑκατὸν δηνάρια, καὶ κρατήσας αὐτὸν ἔπνιγεν λέγων· Ἀπόδος εἴ τι ὀφείλεις. 29 πεσὼν οὖν ὁ σύνδουλος αὐτοῦ παρεκάλει αὐτὸν λέγων· Μακροθύμησον ἐπ' ἐμοί, καὶ ἀποδώσω σοι. 30 ὁ δὲ οὐκ ἤθελεν, ἀλλὰ ἀπελθὼν ἔβαλεν αὐτὸν εἰς φυλακὴν ἕως οὗ ἀποδῷ τὸ ὀφειλόμενον. 31 ἰδόντες οὖν οἱ σύνδουλοι αὐτοῦ τὰ γενόμενα ἐλυπήθησαν σφόδρα, καὶ ἐλθόντες διεσάφησαν τῷ κυρίῳ ἑαυτῶν πάντα τὰ γενόμενα. 32 τότε προσκαλεσάμενος αὐτὸν ὁ κύριος αὐτοῦ λέγει αὐτῷ· Δοῦλε πονηρέ, πᾶσαν τὴν ὀφειλὴν ἐκείνην ἀφῆκά σοι, ἐπεὶ παρεκάλεσάς με· 33 οὐκ ἔδει καὶ σὲ ἐλεῆσαι τὸν σύνδουλόν σου, ὡς κἀγὼ σὲ ἠλέησα; 34 καὶ ὀργισθεὶς ὁ κύριος αὐτοῦ παρέδωκεν αὐτὸν τοῖς βασανισταῖς ἕως οὗ ἀποδῷ πᾶν τὸ ὀφειλόμενον. 35 Οὕτως καὶ ὁ πατήρ μου ὁ οὐράνιος ποιήσει ὑμῖν ἐὰν μὴ ἀφῆτε ἕκαστος τῷ ἀδελφῷ αὐτοῦ ἀπὸ τῶν καρδιῶν ὑμῶν.

Κεφ. ΙΘ´

19:1 Καὶ ἐγένετο ὅτε ἐτέλεσεν ὁ Ἰησοῦς τοὺς λόγους τούτους, μετῆρεν ἀπὸ τῆς Γαλιλαίας καὶ ἦλθεν εἰς τὰ ὅρια τῆς Ἰουδαίας πέραν τοῦ Ἰορδάνου. 2 καὶ ἠκολούθησαν αὐτῷ ὄχλοι πολλοί, καὶ ἐθεράπευσεν αὐτοὺς ἐκεῖ.

26 "Then, falling down, the slave was bowing to him saying, 'Be patient with me, and I shall repay everything to you.' 27 So the lord, having compassion on that slave, released him, and forgave his debt. 28 Now leaving that slave found one of his fellow slaves who was owing him 100 denarii, and grasping him he was choking him saying, 'Pay back what you owe!' 29 Then having fallen down his fellow slave was begging him saying, 'Be patient with me, and I shall repay you.' 30 But he was not willing, rather, departing, he threw him in prison until he should pay back what he owes. 31 Then having seen what happened his fellow slaves were greatly grieved, and going they explained to their lord all that happened. 32 Then having summoned him his lord says to him, 'Evil slave, I forgave you all that debt, because you begged me. 33 Ought you not also to have had mercy on your fellow slave, as I also had mercy on you?' [Yes!] 34 And being enraged his lord handed him over to the jailers until he should pay everything he owed. 35 So also my heavenly Father shall do to you unless you forgive, each one his brother, from your hearts." 19:1 And it happened when Jesus finished these words, he departed from the Galilee and came to the borders of Judea beyond the Jordan. 2 And great crowds followed him, and he healed them there.

Matthew 19:3-12

[3] And Pharisees came toward him testing him and saying, "Is it permitted for a man to divorce his wife for any reason?" [4] So answering back he said, "Have you not read that the creator from the beginning made them male and female [5] and said, 'For this reason a man shall leave his father and mother and be joined to his wife, and the two shall be one flesh?' [Surely, yes!] [6] Therefore, they are no longer two but one flesh. Then that which God joined together let no man separate." [7] They say to him, "Why then did Moses command to give a certificate of divorce and send her away?" [8] He says to them this; "Moses, for your hardened hearts, allowed you to divorce your wives, but from the beginning it has not been so. [9] So, I am saying to you that whoever should divorce his wife not on account of sexual immorality and should marry another commits adultery and he who marries a divorcee commits adultery." [10] The disciples say to him, "If the case of the man with his wife is so, it is not profitable to marry." [11] But he said to them, "Not all accept this word except those to whom it has been given. [12] For there are eunuchs who from the mother's womb were born so, and there are eunuchs who were made eunuchs by people, and there are eunuchs who made themselves eunuchs on account of the Kingdom of the Heavens. He who is able to grasp [this], grasp [it]!

Matthew 19:13-19

[13] Then children were brought to him in order that he might place his hands on them and pray; but the disciples rebuked them. [14] So Jesus said, "Allow the children and do not prevent them to come to me, for the Kingdom of the Heavens [belongs to] such as these." [15] And having laid [his] hands on them he departed from there. [16] And behold! One coming to him said, "Teacher, what good thing should I do that I may have eternal life?" [17] So he said to him, "Why do you ask me about what is good? There is one who is good! But if you wish to enter into life, keep the commands." [18] He says to him, "Which ones?" So Jesus said, "Do not murder, do not commit adultery, do not steal, do not bear false witness, [19] honor your father and mother, and love your neighbor as yourself."

Matthew 19:20-30

[20] The young man says to him, "All of these I kept; yet what do I lack?" [21] Jesus said to him, "If you wish to be mature, go, sell that which you have and give [it] to the poor, and you shall have treasure in the heavens, and come follow me." [22] But having heard the word the young man went away sorrowful, for he had many possessions. [23] So Jesus said to his disciples, "Amen! I am saying to you that it will be difficult for a rich man to enter into the Kingdom of the Heavens; [24] now again I am saying to you, it is easier for a camel to pass through the eye of a needle than for a rich person [to enter] into the kingdom of God." [25] But when the disciples heard [this] they were marveling greatly saying, "Who then is able to be saved?" [26] Now looking at [them], Jesus said to them, "For people this is impossible, but for God everything is possible." [27] Then answering back Peter said to him, "Behold we gave up everything and followed you; what then will be to us?" [28] So Jesus said to them, "Amen! I am saying to you that you who have followed me, in the regeneration, when the Son of Man is seated on his throne of glory, you also shall be seated on 12 thrones judging the 12 tribes of Israel. [29] And everyone who has left houses or brothers or sisters or father or mother or wife or children or fields for the sake of my name, shall receive a hundredfold and inherit eternal life. [30] So, many who are first shall be last and last first."

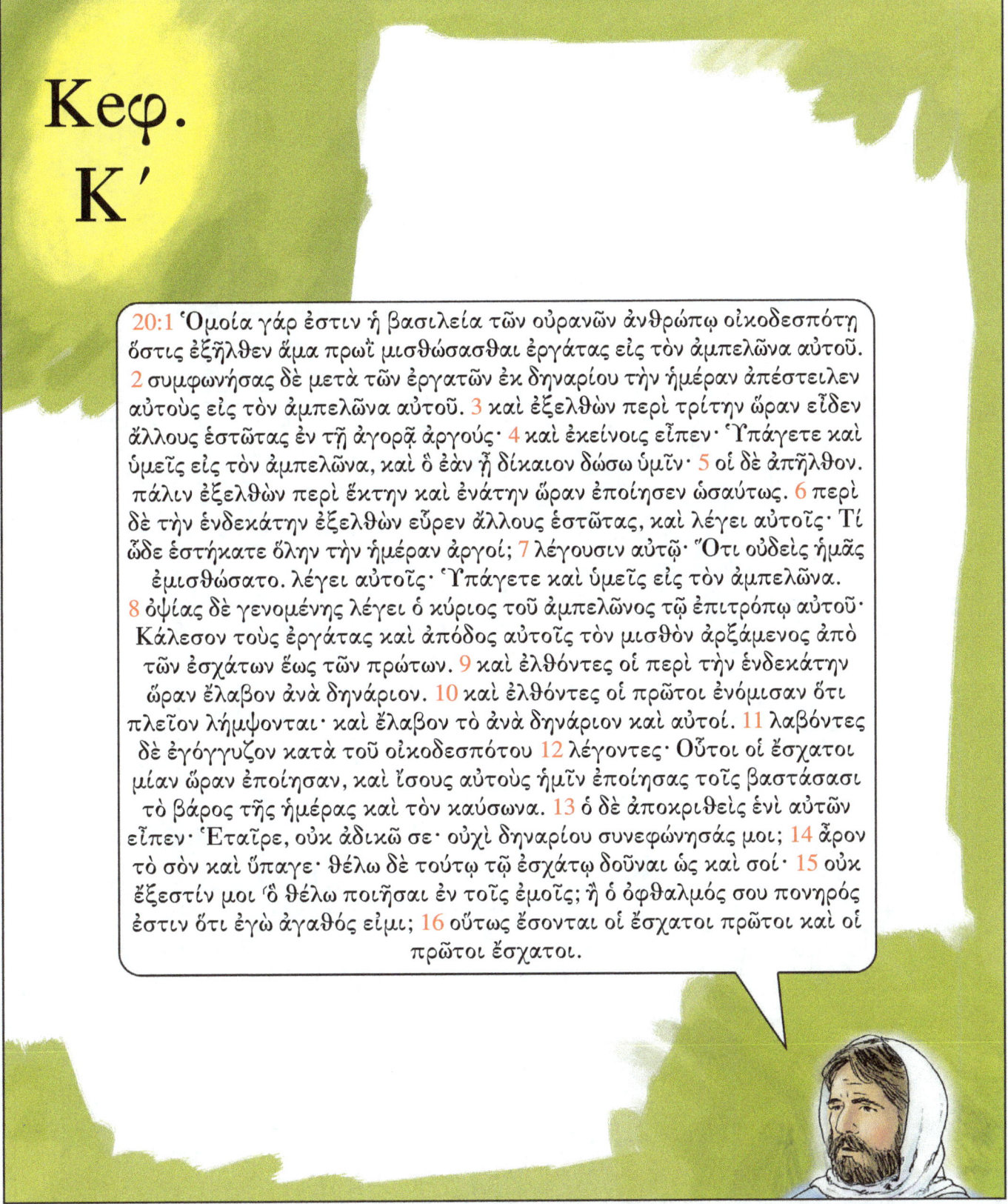

20:1 "For the Kingdom of the Heavens is like a man, a householder, who went out early in the morning to hire workers for his vineyard. ²Now, having agreed with the workers to a denarius per day, he sent them into his vineyard. ³And going out at around the third hour he saw others standing idle in the agora. ⁴And to those he said, 'Go you also into the vineyard, and whatever is just I will give you;' ⁵so they went. Again, going out at around the sixth and ninth hour, he did likewise. ⁶But around the eleventh [hour], going out, he found others standing, and he says to them, 'Why have you been standing idle here all day?' ⁷They say to him, 'Because no one hired us.' He says to them, 'Go you also into the vineyard.' ⁸Now when evening came the master of the vineyard says to his foreman, 'Call the workers and give them the payment beginning with the last until the first.' ⁹And when those from around the eleventh hour came they received one denarius. ¹⁰And when the first ones came they supposed that they would receive more; yet they too received one denarius. ¹¹Now, receiving [it] they were grumbling against the householder ¹²saying, 'These last ones worked one hour, and you made them equal to us who were bearing the burden of the day and the burning heat!' ¹³But answering back [to] one of them he said, 'Friend, I have not been unjust to you; did you not agree with me to a denarius? [Surely, yes!] ¹⁴Take that which is yours and go; but I wish to pay these last ones like you also; ¹⁵is it not right for me to do what I wish with that which is mine? Or is your eye evil because I myself am good?' ¹⁶Thus, the last shall be first and the first last."

Matthew 20:17-26

[17] And going up to Jerusalem Jesus took the 12 disciples aside privately, and on the way he said to the them, [18] "Behold we are going up to Jerusalem, and the Son of Man shall be handed over to the high priests and scribes, and they shall condemn him to death, [19] and they shall hand him over to the Gentiles to mock and scourge and crucify, and on the third day he shall be raised." [20] Then the mother of the sons of Zebedee came toward him with her sons bowing down and asking something of him. [21] So, he said to her, "What do you want?" She says to him, "Say that these two sons of mine may sit one on your right and one on your left in your kingdom." [22] But answering back Jesus said, "You do not know what you are asking; are you able to drink the cup from which I am about to drink?" They say to him, "We are able." [23] He says to them, "You will drink of my cup, but to sit at my right and left is not mine to give, but it is for whom it has been prepared by my Father." [24] And when the ten heard [it] they were indignant with the two brothers. [25] So, Jesus summoning them said, "You know that the rulers of the Gentiles exercise dominion over them and their great men exercise authority over them. [26] It shall not be so with you; but whoever wishes to be great amongst you shall be a servant to you,

Matthew 20:27-21:3

Κεφ. ΚΑ´

[27] and whoever wishes to be first amongst you shall be your servant; [28] just as the Son of Man did not come to be served but to serve and to give his life as a ransom for many." [29] And as they were leaving Jericho a great crowd followed him. [30] And behold two blind men sitting by the road, having heard that Jesus is passing by, cried out saying, "Lord, have mercy on us, Son of David." [31] But the crowd rebuked them to be silent; but they cried out louder saying, "Lord, have mercy on us, Son of David." [32] And stopping Jesus called to them and said, "What do you wish for me to do for you?" [33] They say to him, "Lord, [we wish] that our eyes may be opened." [34] So, being moved with compassion, Jesus touched their eyes, and immediately they gained sight and followed him. 21:1 And when they drew near to Jerusalem and came to Bethphage to the Mount of Olives, then Jesus sent two disciples [2] saying to them, "Go into the village ahead of you, and immediately you will find a donkey tied up and a colt with it; after untying them bring them to me. [3] And if someone says something to you, you shall say this: 'The Lord has need of them;' so he shall send them at once."

Matthew 21:4-11

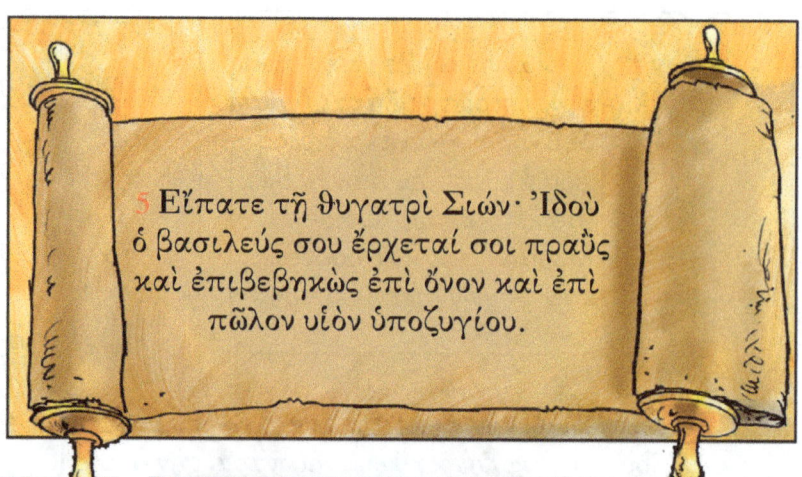

[4] Now this has happened in order that what was spoken through the prophet would be fulfilled saying, [5] "Say to the Daughter of Zion; 'behold your king is coming to you gentle and riding on a donkey and on a colt the foal of a pack animal.'" [6] So, the disciples going and doing just as Jesus ordered them, [7] led the donkey and the colt, and they laid their garments on them, and he sat upon them. [8] Now a very large crowd spread their own garments on the road, moreover others were cutting branches from the trees and were spreading [them] on the road. [9] Now the crowds that were going in front of him and that were following him kept crying out saying, "Hosanna to the Son of David; blessed is the one who comes in the name of the LORD; Hosanna in the highest." [10] And entering into Jerusalem the whole city was shaken saying, "Who is this?" [11] Now, the crowds were saying, "This is the prophet Jesus who [is] from Nazareth of the Galilee."

Matthew 21:12-19

12 Καὶ εἰσῆλθεν Ἰησοῦς εἰς τὸ ἱερόν, καὶ ἐξέβαλεν πάντας τοὺς πωλοῦντας καὶ ἀγοράζοντας ἐν τῷ ἱερῷ καὶ τὰς τραπέζας τῶν κολλυβιστῶν κατέστρεψεν καὶ τὰς καθέδρας τῶν πωλούντων τὰς περιστεράς **13** καὶ λέγει αὐτοῖς·

Γέγραπται· Ὁ οἶκός μου οἶκος προσευχῆς κληθήσεται, ὑμεῖς δὲ αὐτὸν ποιεῖτε σπήλαιον λῃστῶν.

14 Καὶ προσῆλθον αὐτῷ τυφλοὶ καὶ χωλοὶ ἐν τῷ ἱερῷ, καὶ ἐθεράπευσεν αὐτούς. **15** ἰδόντες δὲ οἱ ἀρχιερεῖς καὶ οἱ γραμματεῖς τὰ θαυμάσια ἃ ἐποίησεν καὶ τοὺς παῖδας τοὺς κράζοντας ἐν τῷ ἱερῷ καὶ λέγοντας· Ὡσαννὰ τῷ υἱῷ Δαυίδ ἠγανάκτησαν **16** καὶ εἶπαν αὐτῷ· Ἀκούεις τί οὗτοι λέγουσιν;

ὁ δὲ Ἰησοῦς λέγει αὐτοῖς·

Ναί. οὐδέποτε ἀνέγνωτε ὅτι Ἐκ στόματος νηπίων καὶ θηλαζόντων κατηρτίσω αἶνον;

17 καὶ καταλιπὼν αὐτοὺς ἐξῆλθεν ἔξω τῆς πόλεως εἰς Βηθανίαν, καὶ ηὐλίσθη ἐκεῖ.

18 Πρωῒ δὲ ἐπανάγων εἰς τὴν πόλιν ἐπείνασεν. **19** καὶ ἰδὼν συκῆν μίαν ἐπὶ τῆς ὁδοῦ ἦλθεν ἐπ' αὐτήν, καὶ οὐδὲν εὗρεν ἐν αὐτῇ εἰ μὴ φύλλα μόνον, καὶ λέγει αὐτῇ·

Μηκέτι ἐκ σοῦ καρπὸς γένηται εἰς τὸν αἰῶνα·

καὶ ἐξηράνθη παραχρῆμα ἡ συκῆ.

[12] And Jesus went into the temple, and he cast out all who were selling and buying in the temple and the tables of the moneychangers he overturned even the chairs of those selling doves, [13] and says to them, "It has been written, 'My house shall be called a house of prayer,' but you make it a den of robbers!" [14] And blind and lame came to him in the temple, and he healed them. [15] But when the chief priests and scribes saw the wonders which he did and the children who were crying out in the temple and saying, "Hosanna to the Son of David" they were indignant [16] and said to him, "Do you hear what they are saying?" So Jesus says to them, "Yes. Have you never read this: 'Out of the mouths of young children and infants you have prepared praise?'" [Surely, yes!] [17] And leaving them he went out of the city to Bethany, and he spent the night there. [18] But in the morning when he returned to the city he was hungry. [19] And having seen a fig tree by the road he went to it, and found on it nothing except leaves alone, and he says to it, "May fruit never again come from you;" and the fig tree dried up immediately.

Matthew 21:20-27

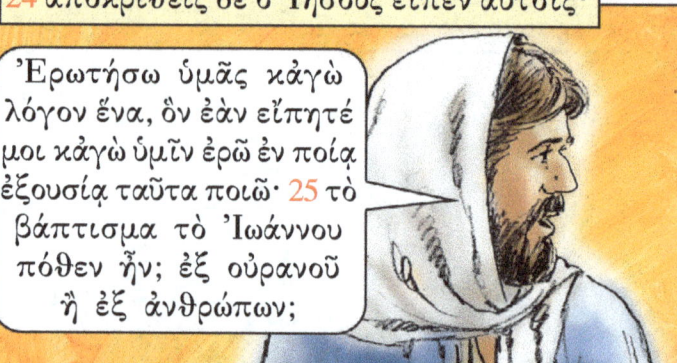

[20] And seeing [this] the disciples were astonished saying, "How did the fig tree wither immediately?" [21] So answering Jesus said to them, "Amen! I am saying to you, if you have faith and do not doubt, you shall do not only what was done to this fig tree, but you may even say to this mountain, 'be taken up and cast into the sea,' it will be done. [22] And all things you ask for in prayer, believing, you shall receive." [23] And after he entered the temple the chief priests and elders of the people approached him while teaching saying, "By what authority are you doing these things? And who gave you this authority?" [24] So answering back Jesus said to them, "I also will ask you about one matter, which if you tell me I will also tell you by what authority I do these things; [25] the baptism of John where was it from? From heaven or from humans?" Now they were debating amongst themselves saying, "If we say from heaven he will say to us; 'why then did you not believe him?' [26] But if we say from humans, we fear the crowd, for all hold John as a prophet." [27] And answering back to Jesus they said, "We do not know."

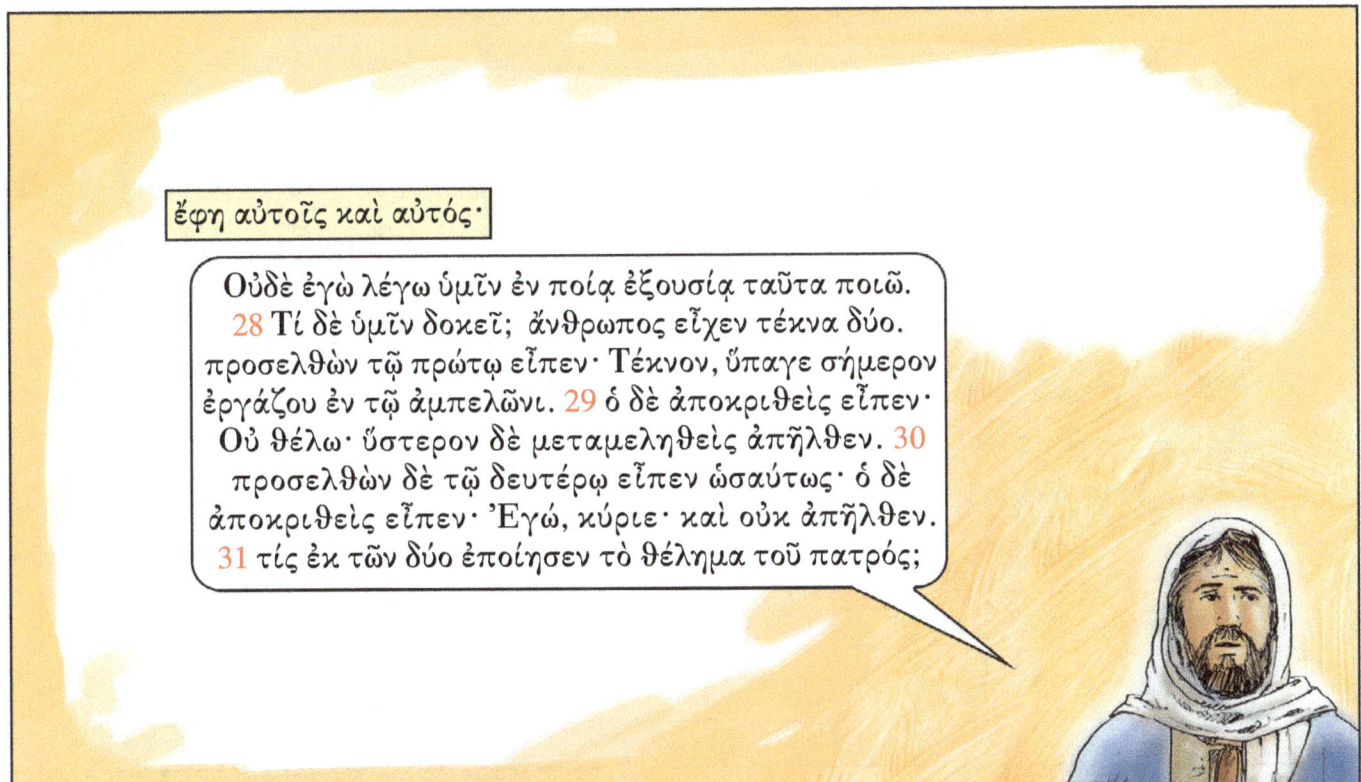

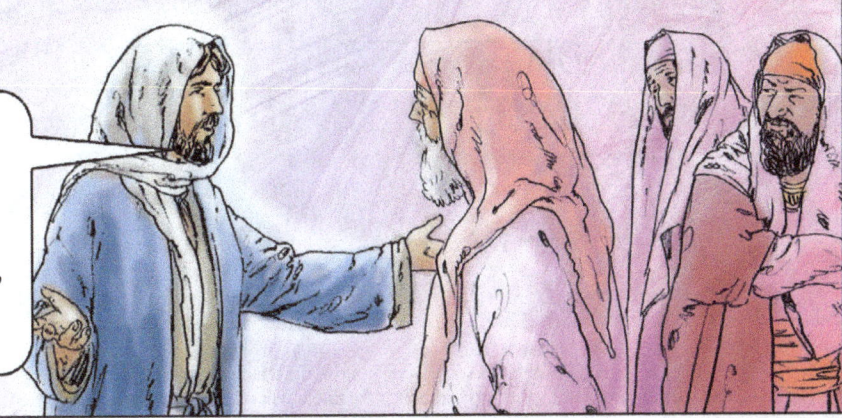

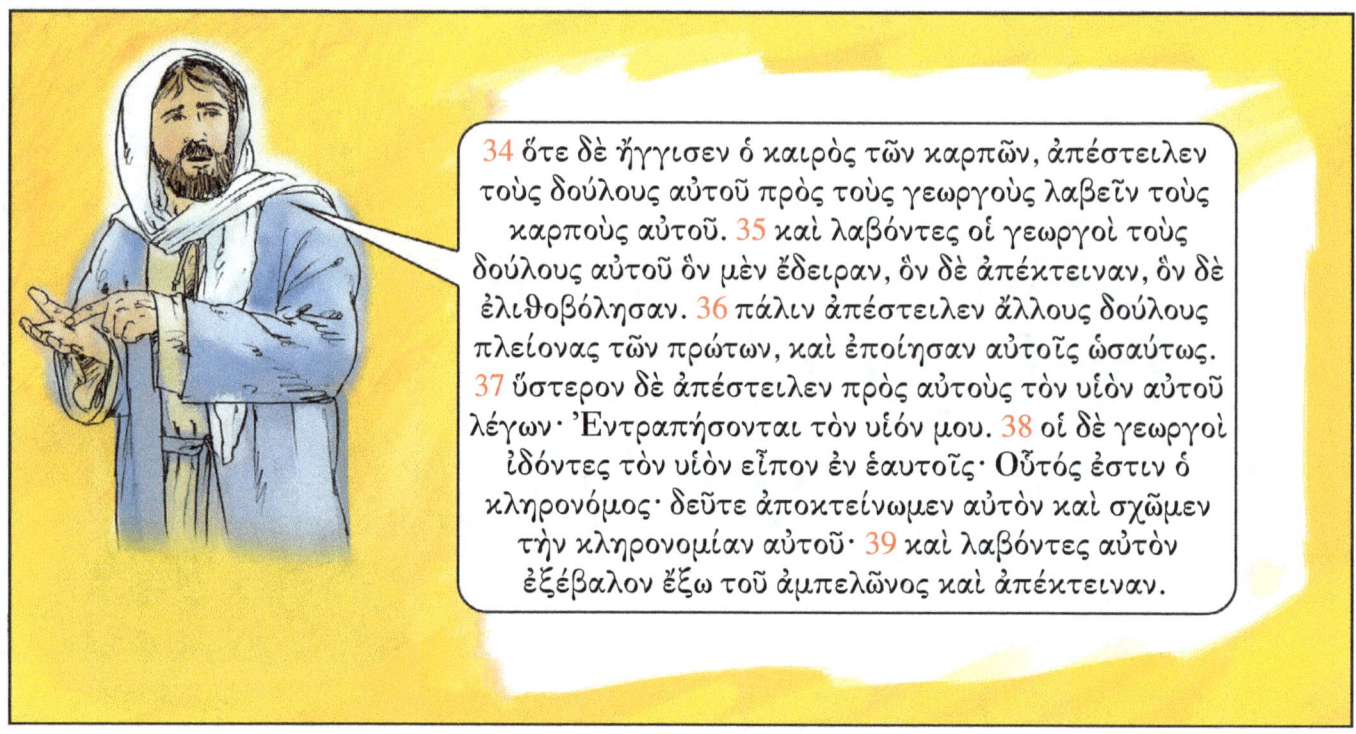

Matthew 21:34-43

34 "So when the season of the fruits drew near, he sent his servants to the tenant farmers to get his fruits. 35 And when the tenant farmers received his servants they whipped one, but another they killed, moreover another they stoned. 36 Again he sent other servants more than the first ones, and they did to them likewise. 37 But afterwards he sent to them his son saying, 'They will respect my son.' 38 But when the tenant farmers saw the son they said to each other; 'This is the heir; come let us kill him and we have his inheritance;' 39 and seizing him they threw him out of the vineyard and killed [him]. 40 Then when the Lord of the vineyard comes, what shall he do to those tenant farmers?" 41 They say to him, "Those bad people he will destroy severely, and the vineyard he will lease out to other tenant farmers, who will give back to him the fruits in their seasons." 42 Jesus says to them, "Have you never read in the Scriptures; 'The Stone which the builders rejected this one became [the] head of [the] corner; this came from the LORD, and it is marvelous in our eyes?' [Surely, yes!] 43 Because of this I am saying to you that the kingdom of God shall be taken from you and given to a people producing its fruits."

Matthew 21:43-22:6

44 Καὶ ὁ πεσὼν ἐπὶ τὸν λίθον τοῦτον συνθλασθήσεται· ἐφ ὃν δ' ἂν πέσῃ λικμήσει αὐτόν

45 Καὶ ἀκούσαντες οἱ ἀρχιερεῖς καὶ οἱ Φαρισαῖοι τὰς παραβολὰς αὐτοῦ ἔγνωσαν ὅτι περὶ αὐτῶν λέγει· 46 καὶ ζητοῦντες αὐτὸν κρατῆσαι ἐφοβήθησαν τοὺς ὄχλους, ἐπεὶ εἰς προφήτην αὐτὸν εἶχον.

Κεφ. ΚΒ΄

22:1 Καὶ ἀποκριθεὶς ὁ Ἰησοῦς πάλιν εἶπεν ἐν παραβολαῖς αὐτοῖς λέγων·

2 Ὡμοιώθη ἡ βασιλεία τῶν οὐρανῶν ἀνθρώπῳ βασιλεῖ, ὅστις ἐποίησεν γάμους τῷ υἱῷ αὐτοῦ. 3 καὶ ἀπέστειλεν τοὺς δούλους αὐτοῦ καλέσαι τοὺς κεκλημένους εἰς τοὺς γάμους, καὶ οὐκ ἤθελον ἐλθεῖν. 4 πάλιν ἀπέστειλεν ἄλλους δούλους λέγων· Εἴπατε τοῖς κεκλημένοις· Ἰδοὺ τὸ ἄριστόν μου ἡτοίμακα, οἱ ταῦροί μου καὶ τὰ σιτιστὰ τεθυμένα, καὶ πάντα ἕτοιμα· δεῦτε εἰς τοὺς γάμους. 5 οἱ δὲ ἀμελήσαντες ἀπῆλθον, ὃς μὲν εἰς τὸν ἴδιον ἀγρόν, ὃς δὲ ἐπὶ τὴν ἐμπορίαν αὐτοῦ· 6 οἱ δὲ λοιποὶ κρατήσαντες τοὺς δούλους αὐτοῦ ὕβρισαν καὶ ἀπέκτειναν.

44 "And he who is falling on this stone shall be crushed; so on whoever it might fall it shall destroy him." 45 And having heard his parables the chief priests and Pharisees realized that he speaks about them; 46 and seeking to grasp him they feared the crowds, since they were holding him as a prophet. 22:1 And answering Jesus again spoke in parables to them saying, 2 "The Kingdom of the Heavens is like a man, a king, who gave a wedding feast for his son. 3 And he sent his servants to call those who had been invited to the wedding feast, and they were not willing to come. 4 Again he sent other servants saying, "Say to those have been called; 'Behold I have prepared my dinner, my bulls and fattened calves have been killed, and everything is ready; come to the wedding feast!' 5 But ignoring them they went away, one to his own field, another one to his business; 6 but the others, seizing his servants, mistreated and killed [them]."

Matthew 22:7-17

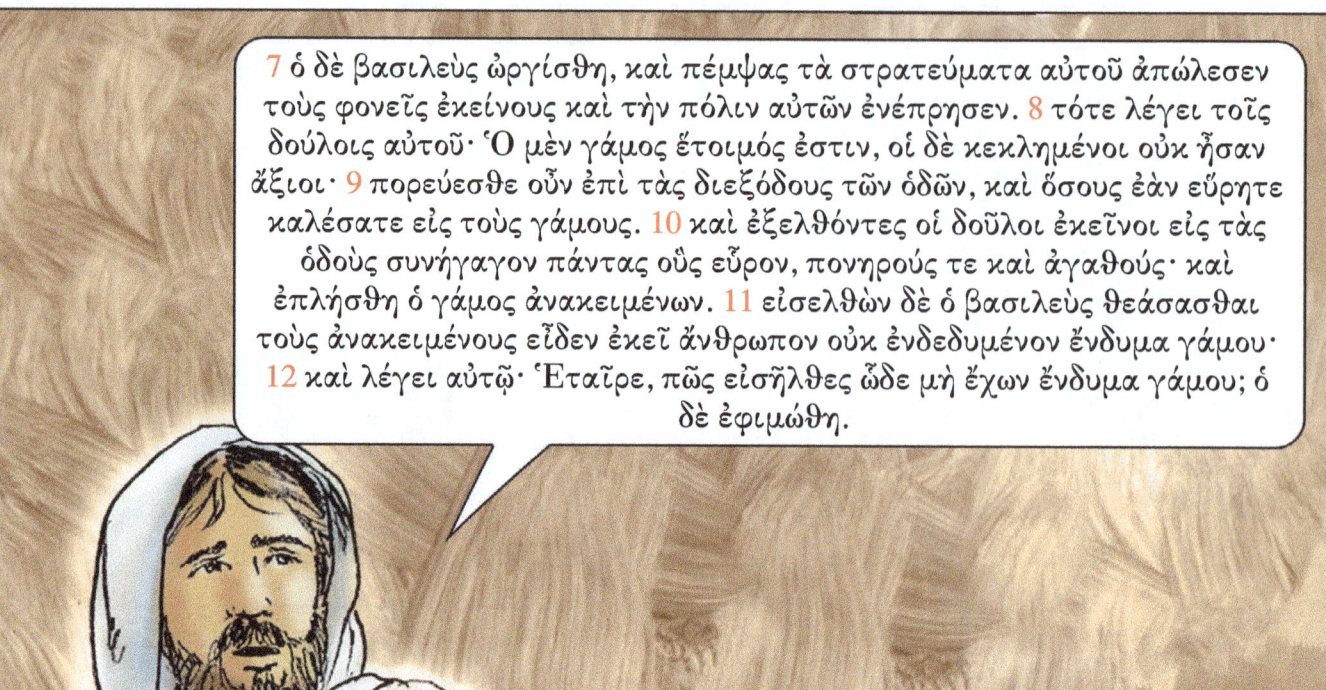

[7] "Now the king was enraged and, sending forth his soldiers, he destroyed those murderers and set fire to their city. [8] Then he says to his servants, 'The wedding feast is ready, but those invited were not worthy; [9] go therefore to where the roads leave the city, and as many as you find invite to the wedding feast.' [10] And having gone out on those roads the servants gathered everyone they found, both evil and good; and the wedding feast was filled with those reclining at the tables. [11] But the king, entering to behold those reclining, saw a man not wearing a wedding garment; [12] and he says to him, 'Friend, how did you enter here not having a wedding garment?' But the man was speechless. [13] Then the king said to the servants, 'Bind his feet and hands to cast him out into the outer darkness; in that place there shall be weeping and gnashing of teeth. [14] For many are invited but few are chosen.' [15] Then, departing, the Pharisees plotted in order that they might entrap him with a word. [16] And they send to him their disciples with the Herodians saying, "Teacher, we know that you are truthful and teach the way of God in truthfulness, and there is not a concern for you about anyone, for you do not look at the reputation of people; [17] then tell us how does it seem to you; is it lawful to pay a poll tax to Caesar or not?"

Matthew 22:18-28

[18] But knowing their wickedness Jesus said, "Why do you test me, hypocrites? [19] Show me the poll-tax coin!" So they brought him a denarius. [20] And he says to them, "Whose is this image and the inscription?" [21] They say to him, "Caesar's." Then he says to them, "Give back then the things of Caesar to Caesar and the things of God to God." [22] And when they heard [this] they were marveling, and leaving him they went away. [23] On that day Sadducees came to him, those who say there is no resurrection, and they questioned him [24] saying, "Teacher, Moses said; 'If someone dies not having a child, his brother shall marry his wife and raise up a descendant for his brother.' [25] Now there were seven brothers with us; and the first, marrying, died, and not having a descendant he left his wife to his brother; [26] and the second likewise and the third, until the seventh; [27] now last of all the wife died. [28] In the resurrection, then, to which of the seven shall she be a wife? For they all had her."

Matthew 22:29-40

29 Ἀποκριθεὶς δὲ ὁ Ἰησοῦς εἶπεν αὐτοῖς·

Πλανᾶσθε μὴ εἰδότες τὰς γραφὰς μηδὲ τὴν δύναμιν τοῦ θεοῦ· **30** ἐν γὰρ τῇ ἀναστάσει οὔτε γαμοῦσιν οὔτε γαμίζονται, ἀλλ' ὡς ἄγγελοι θεοῦ ἐν τῷ οὐρανῷ εἰσιν· **31** περὶ δὲ τῆς ἀναστάσεως τῶν νεκρῶν οὐκ ἀνέγνωτε τὸ ῥηθὲν ὑμῖν ὑπὸ τοῦ θεοῦ λέγοντος· **32** Ἐγώ εἰμι ὁ θεὸς Ἀβραὰμ καὶ ὁ θεὸς Ἰσαὰκ καὶ ὁ θεὸς Ἰακώβ; οὐκ ἔστιν ὁ θεὸς νεκρῶν ἀλλὰ ζώντων.

33 καὶ ἀκούσαντες οἱ ὄχλοι ἐξεπλήσσοντο ἐπὶ τῇ διδαχῇ αὐτοῦ. **34** Οἱ δὲ Φαρισαῖοι ἀκούσαντες ὅτι ἐφίμωσεν τοὺς Σαδδουκαίους συνήχθησαν ἐπὶ τὸ αὐτό. **35** καὶ ἐπηρώτησεν εἷς ἐξ αὐτῶν νομικὸς πειράζων αὐτόν·

36 Διδάσκαλε, ποία ἐντολὴ μεγάλη ἐν τῷ νόμῳ; **37** ὁ δὲ ἔφη αὐτῷ·

Ἀγαπήσεις κύριον τὸν θεόν σου ἐν ὅλῃ τῇ καρδίᾳ σου καὶ ἐν ὅλῃ τῇ ψυχῇ σου καὶ ἐν ὅλῃ τῇ διανοίᾳ σου· **38** αὕτη ἐστὶν ἡ μεγάλη καὶ πρώτη ἐντολή. **39** Δευτέρα δὲ ὁμοία αὐτῇ· Ἀγαπήσεις τὸν πλησίον σου ὡς σεαυτόν. **40** ἐν ταύταις ταῖς δυσὶν ἐντολαῖς ὅλος ὁ νόμος κρέμαται καὶ οἱ προφῆται.

29 So answering back Jesus said to them, "You are being led astray not knowing the Scriptures nor the power of God; **30** for in the resurrection they neither marry nor are given in marriage, but they are as the angels of God in the heavens; **31** so concerning the resurrection from the dead did you not read that which was spoken to you by God saying, **32** 'I am the God of Abraham and the God of Isaac and the God of Jacob?' [Surely, yes!] He is not the God of the dead but of the living." **33** And hearing [this] the crowds were astonished by his teaching. **34** But the Pharisees, having heard that he had silenced the Sadducees, came together in the same place. **35** And one of them, a lawyer, questioned him to trap him, **36** "Teacher, which commandment is the greatest in the Law?" **37** So Jesus said to him, "'You shall love the LORD your God with all your heart and with all your soul and with all your mind'; **38** this is the greatest and the first commandment. **39** But the second is like it, 'You shall love your neighbor as yourself.' **40** On these two commandments hang the whole law and the prophets."

Matthew 22:41-23:3

Κεφ. ΚΓ΄

[41] But while the Pharisees were gathered together Jesus questioned them [42] saying, "What do you think about the Messiah? Whose son is he?" They say to him; "David's." [43] He says to them, "How then does David by the Spirit call him Lord saying; [44] 'The Lord said to my Lord; sit at my right hand until I put your enemies beneath your feet?' [45] If then David calls him Lord, how is he his son?" [46] And no one was able to answer him a word, nor dared anyone from that day on question him anymore. 23:1 Then Jesus spoke to the crowds and his disciples [2] saying, "The scribes and Pharisees have taken their seat on the chair of Moses. [3] Everything then, as much as they say, do and keep, but according to their works do not do; for they speak and do not do [it]."

Matthew 23:4-22

4 δεσμεύουσιν δὲ φορτία βαρέα καὶ ἐπιτιθέασιν ἐπὶ τοὺς ὤμους τῶν ἀνθρώπων, αὐτοὶ δὲ τῷ δακτύλῳ αὐτῶν οὐ θέλουσιν κινῆσαι αὐτά. 5 πάντα δὲ τὰ ἔργα αὐτῶν ποιοῦσιν πρὸς τὸ θεαθῆναι τοῖς ἀνθρώποις· πλατύνουσι γὰρ τὰ φυλακτήρια αὐτῶν καὶ μεγαλύνουσι τὰ κράσπεδα, 6 φιλοῦσι δὲ τὴν πρωτοκλισίαν ἐν τοῖς δείπνοις καὶ τὰς πρωτοκαθεδρίας ἐν ταῖς συναγωγαῖς 7 καὶ τοὺς ἀσπασμοὺς ἐν ταῖς ἀγοραῖς καὶ καλεῖσθαι ὑπὸ τῶν ἀνθρώπων· Ῥαββί. 8 ὑμεῖς δὲ μὴ κληθῆτε· Ῥαββί, εἷς γάρ ἐστιν ὑμῶν ὁ διδάσκαλος, πάντες δὲ ὑμεῖς ἀδελφοί ἐστε· 9 καὶ πατέρα μὴ καλέσητε ὑμῶν ἐπὶ τῆς γῆς, εἷς γάρ ἐστιν ὑμῶν ὁ πατὴρ ὁ οὐράνιος· 10 μηδὲ κληθῆτε καθηγηταί, ὅτι καθηγητὴς ὑμῶν ἐστιν εἷς ὁ χριστός· 11 ὁ δὲ μείζων ὑμῶν ἔσται ὑμῶν διάκονος. 12 ὅστις δὲ ὑψώσει ἑαυτὸν ταπεινωθήσεται, καὶ ὅστις ταπεινώσει ἑαυτὸν ὑψωθήσεται. 13 Οὐαὶ δὲ ὑμῖν, γραμματεῖς καὶ Φαρισαῖοι ὑποκριταί, ὅτι κλείετε τὴν βασιλείαν τῶν οὐρανῶν ἔμπροσθεν τῶν ἀνθρώπων· ὑμεῖς γὰρ οὐκ εἰσέρχεσθε, οὐδὲ τοὺς εἰσερχομένους ἀφίετε εἰσελθεῖν. 15 Οὐαὶ ὑμῖν, γραμματεῖς καὶ Φαρισαῖοι ὑποκριταί, ὅτι περιάγετε τὴν θάλασσαν καὶ τὴν ξηρὰν ποιῆσαι ἕνα προσήλυτον, καὶ ὅταν γένηται ποιεῖτε αὐτὸν υἱὸν γεέννης διπλότερον ὑμῶν. 16 Οὐαὶ ὑμῖν, ὁδηγοὶ τυφλοὶ οἱ λέγοντες· Ὃς ἂν ὀμόσῃ ἐν τῷ ναῷ, οὐδέν ἐστιν, ὃς δ᾽ ἂν ὀμόσῃ ἐν τῷ χρυσῷ τοῦ ναοῦ ὀφείλει. 17 μωροὶ καὶ τυφλοί, τίς γὰρ μείζων ἐστίν, ὁ χρυσὸς ἢ ὁ ναὸς ὁ ἁγιάσας τὸν χρυσόν; 18 καί· Ὃς ἂν ὀμόσῃ ἐν τῷ θυσιαστηρίῳ, οὐδέν ἐστιν, ὃς δ᾽ ἂν ὀμόσῃ ἐν τῷ δώρῳ τῷ ἐπάνω αὐτοῦ ὀφείλει. 19 τυφλοί, τί γὰρ μεῖζον, τὸ δῶρον ἢ τὸ θυσιαστήριον τὸ ἁγιάζον τὸ δῶρον; 20 ὁ οὖν ὀμόσας ἐν τῷ θυσιαστηρίῳ ὀμνύει ἐν αὐτῷ καὶ ἐν πᾶσι τοῖς ἐπάνω αὐτοῦ· 21 καὶ ὁ ὀμόσας ἐν τῷ ναῷ ὀμνύει ἐν αὐτῷ καὶ ἐν τῷ κατοικοῦντι αὐτόν· 22 καὶ ὁ ὀμόσας ἐν τῷ οὐρανῷ ὀμνύει ἐν τῷ θρόνῳ τοῦ θεοῦ καὶ ἐν τῷ καθημένῳ ἐπάνω αὐτοῦ.

4 "Moreover, they bind together heavy burdens and place them upon people's shoulders, but with their finger they do not wish to move them. 5 Now they do all their deeds to be seen by people; for they enlarge their phylacteries and lengthen the tassels. 6 Additionally, they love the place of honor at dinners and chief seats in the synagogues 7 and the salutations in the agoras and to be called 'Rabbi' by the people. 8 But you yourselves should not be called 'Rabbi,' for one is your teacher, so all of you are brothers; 9 and you should not call [anyone] father on earth, for one is your father in heaven; 10 nor should you be called leaders, for one is your leader, the Messiah; 11 but the greatest of you shall be your servant, 12 so whoever shall exalt himself shall be humbled, and whoever shall humble himself shall be exalted. 13 But woe to you, scribes and Pharisees, hypocrites, for you are shutting the Kingdom of the Heavens before people; for you yourselves do not enter, nor do you allow those who are entering to enter. 15 Woe to you, scribes and Pharisees, hypocrites, for you go around sea and dry land to make one proselyte, and when it happens you make him twice as much a son of Gehenna as yourselves. 16 Woe to you, blind guides who are saying, 'Whoever swears by the Temple, that is nothing, but whoever swears by the gold of the Temple he is obligated.' 17 Fools and blind men! For what is greater, the gold or the Temple which sanctifies the gold? 18 Also, 'Whoever swears by the altar, that is nothing, but whoever swears by the gift upon it is obligated.' 19 Blind men, for what is greater, the gift or the alter which sanctifies the gift? 20 Then the one swearing by the altar is swearing by it and everything upon it; 21 and the one swearing by the Temple he swears by it and the one who dwells in it; 22 and the one who swears by heaven swears by the throne of God and by the one seated upon it."

Matthew 23:23-39

23 Οὐαὶ ὑμῖν, γραμματεῖς καὶ Φαρισαῖοι ὑποκριταί, ὅτι ἀποδεκατοῦτε τὸ ἡδύοσμον καὶ τὸ ἄνηθον καὶ τὸ κύμινον, καὶ ἀφήκατε τὰ βαρύτερα τοῦ νόμου, τὴν κρίσιν καὶ τὸ ἔλεος καὶ τὴν πίστιν· ταῦτα ἔδει ποιῆσαι κἀκεῖνα μὴ ἀφιέναι. 24 ὁδηγοὶ τυφλοί, οἱ διϋλίζοντες τὸν κώνωπα τὴν δὲ κάμηλον καταπίνοντες. 25 Οὐαὶ ὑμῖν, γραμματεῖς καὶ Φαρισαῖοι ὑποκριταί, ὅτι καθαρίζετε τὸ ἔξωθεν τοῦ ποτηρίου καὶ τῆς παροψίδος, ἔσωθεν δὲ γέμουσιν ἐξ ἁρπαγῆς καὶ ἀκρασίας. 26 Φαρισαῖε τυφλέ, καθάρισον πρῶτον τὸ ἐντὸς τοῦ ποτηρίου καὶ τῆς παροψίδος, ἵνα γένηται καὶ τὸ ἐκτὸς αὐτοῦ καθαρόν. 27 Οὐαὶ ὑμῖν, γραμματεῖς καὶ Φαρισαῖοι ὑποκριταί, ὅτι παρομοιάζετε τάφοις κεκονιαμένοις, οἵτινες ἔξωθεν μὲν φαίνονται ὡραῖοι ἔσωθεν δὲ γέμουσιν ὀστέων νεκρῶν καὶ πάσης ἀκαθαρσίας· 28 οὕτως καὶ ὑμεῖς ἔξωθεν μὲν φαίνεσθε τοῖς ἀνθρώποις δίκαιοι, ἔσωθεν δέ ἐστε μεστοὶ ὑποκρίσεως καὶ ἀνομίας. 29 Οὐαὶ ὑμῖν, γραμματεῖς καὶ Φαρισαῖοι ὑποκριταί, ὅτι οἰκοδομεῖτε τοὺς τάφους τῶν προφητῶν καὶ κοσμεῖτε τὰ μνημεῖα τῶν δικαίων, 30 καὶ λέγετε· Εἰ ἤμεθα ἐν ταῖς ἡμέραις τῶν πατέρων ἡμῶν, οὐκ ἂν ἤμεθα αὐτῶν κοινωνοὶ ἐν τῷ αἵματι τῶν προφητῶν· 31 ὥστε μαρτυρεῖτε ἑαυτοῖς ὅτι υἱοί ἐστε τῶν φονευσάντων τοὺς προφήτας. 32 καὶ ὑμεῖς πληρώσατε τὸ μέτρον τῶν πατέρων ὑμῶν. 33 ὄφεις γεννήματα ἐχιδνῶν, πῶς φύγητε ἀπὸ τῆς κρίσεως τῆς γεέννης; 34 διὰ τοῦτο ἰδοὺ ἐγὼ ἀποστέλλω πρὸς ὑμᾶς προφήτας καὶ σοφοὺς καὶ γραμματεῖς· ἐξ αὐτῶν ἀποκτενεῖτε καὶ σταυρώσετε, καὶ ἐξ αὐτῶν μαστιγώσετε ἐν ταῖς συναγωγαῖς ὑμῶν καὶ διώξετε ἀπὸ πόλεως εἰς πόλιν· 35 ὅπως ἔλθῃ ἐφ' ὑμᾶς πᾶν αἷμα δίκαιον ἐκχυννόμενον ἐπὶ τῆς γῆς ἀπὸ τοῦ αἵματος Ἄβελ τοῦ δικαίου ἕως τοῦ αἵματος Ζαχαρίου υἱοῦ Βαραχίου, ὃν ἐφονεύσατε μεταξὺ τοῦ ναοῦ καὶ τοῦ θυσιαστηρίου. 36 ἀμὴν λέγω ὑμῖν, ἥξει ταῦτα πάντα ἐπὶ τὴν γενεὰν ταύτην. 37 Ἰερουσαλὴμ Ἰερουσαλήμ, ἡ ἀποκτείνουσα τοὺς προφήτας καὶ λιθοβολοῦσα τοὺς ἀπεσταλμένους πρὸς αὐτήν — ποσάκις ἠθέλησα ἐπισυναγαγεῖν τὰ τέκνα σου, ὃν τρόπον ὄρνις ἐπισυνάγει τὰ νοσσία αὐτῆς ὑπὸ τὰς πτέρυγας, καὶ οὐκ ἠθελήσατε; 38 ἰδοὺ ἀφίεται ὑμῖν ὁ οἶκος ὑμῶν ἔρημος. 39 λέγω γὰρ ὑμῖν, οὐ μή με ἴδητε ἀπ' ἄρτι ἕως ἂν εἴπητε· Εὐλογημένος ὁ ἐρχόμενος ἐν ὀνόματι κυρίου.

23 "Woe to you, scribes and Pharisees, hypocrites, for you tithe mint and dill and cumin, and you neglected the weightier matters of the Law, justice and mercy and faithfulness; these things it was necessary to do and those things not to neglect. 24 Blind guides, who are straining out the gnat but swallowing a camel! 25 Woe to you, scribes and Pharisees, hypocrites, for you clean the outside of the cup and plate, but on the inside they are full of robbery and self-indulgence! 26 Blind Pharisee, cleanse first the inside of the cup and the plate, so that the outside may be clean also. 27 Woe to you, scribes and Pharisees, hypocrites, for you are like whitewashed tombs, which appear beautiful from the outside but on the inside they are full of bones of the dead and every impurity; 28 similarly also you on the outside appear righteous to people, but on the inside you are full of hypocrisy and lawlessness. 29 Woe to you, scribes and Pharisees, hypocrites, for you build the graves of the prophets and adorn the tombs of the righteous, 30 and you say, 'If we had been alive in the days of our fathers, we would not have been partners with them in the blood of the prophets;' 31 for this reason you testify against yourselves that you are sons of those who killed the prophets. 32 And you fill up the measure of your fathers. 33 Snakes! Brood of vipers! How will you escape the judgment of Gehenna? 34 Because of this behold I am sending you prophets and wise men and scribes; some of whom you will kill and crucify, and some of whom you will scourge in your synagogues and persecute from city to city; 35 in order that upon you may come all the righteous blood being poured out upon the earth from the blood of Abel the righteous until the blood of Zechariah son of Barachiah, whom you murdered between the Temple and the altar. 36 Amen! I am saying to you, all these things shall come upon this generation. 37 Jerusalem Jerusalem, who kills the prophets and stones those sent to her – how often I wished to gather your children, like a hen gathers her young under the wings, and you did not want to. 38 Behold your house is left to you desolate. 39 For I am saying to you, you will certainly not see me from now on until you say, 'Blessed is the one coming in the name of the LORD.'"

Matthew 24:1-14

Κεφ. ΚΔ΄

24:1 Καὶ ἐξελθὼν ὁ Ἰησοῦς ἀπὸ τοῦ ἱεροῦ ἐπορεύετο, καὶ προσῆλθον οἱ μαθηταὶ αὐτοῦ ἐπιδεῖξαι αὐτῷ τὰς οἰκοδομὰς τοῦ ἱεροῦ· 2 ὁ δὲ ἀποκριθεὶς εἶπεν αὐτοῖς·

Οὐ βλέπετε ταῦτα πάντα; ἀμὴν λέγω ὑμῖν, οὐ μὴ ἀφεθῇ ὧδε λίθος ἐπὶ λίθον ὃς οὐ καταλυθήσεται.

3 Καθημένου δὲ αὐτοῦ ἐπὶ τοῦ Ὄρους τῶν Ἐλαιῶν προσῆλθον αὐτῷ οἱ μαθηταὶ κατ' ἰδίαν λέγοντες·

Εἰπὸν ἡμῖν πότε ταῦτα ἔσται, καὶ τί τὸ σημεῖον τῆς σῆς παρουσίας καὶ συντελείας τοῦ αἰῶνος.

4 καὶ ἀποκριθεὶς ὁ Ἰησοῦς εἶπεν αὐτοῖς·

Βλέπετε μή τις ὑμᾶς πλανήσῃ· 5 πολλοὶ γὰρ ἐλεύσονται ἐπὶ τῷ ὀνόματί μου λέγοντες· Ἐγώ εἰμι ὁ χριστός, καὶ πολλοὺς πλανήσουσιν. 6 μελλήσετε δὲ ἀκούειν πολέμους καὶ ἀκοὰς πολέμων· ὁρᾶτε, μὴ θροεῖσθε· δεῖ γὰρ γενέσθαι, ἀλλ' οὔπω ἐστὶν τὸ τέλος. 7 ἐγερθήσεται γὰρ ἔθνος ἐπὶ ἔθνος καὶ βασιλεία ἐπὶ βασιλείαν, καὶ ἔσονται λιμοὶ καὶ σεισμοὶ κατὰ τόπους· 8 πάντα δὲ ταῦτα ἀρχὴ ὠδίνων. 9 Τότε παραδώσουσιν ὑμᾶς εἰς θλῖψιν καὶ ἀποκτενοῦσιν ὑμᾶς, καὶ ἔσεσθε μισούμενοι ὑπὸ πάντων τῶν ἐθνῶν διὰ τὸ ὄνομά μου. 10 καὶ τότε σκανδαλισθήσονται πολλοὶ καὶ ἀλλήλους παραδώσουσιν καὶ μισήσουσιν ἀλλήλους· 11 καὶ πολοὶ ψευδοπροφῆται ἐγερθήσονται καὶ πλανήσουσιν πολλούς· 12 καὶ διὰ τὸ πληθυνθῆναι τὴν ἀνομίαν ψυγήσεται ἡ ἀγάπη τῶν πολλῶν. 13 ὁ δὲ ὑπομείνας εἰς τέλος οὗτος σωθήσεται. 14 καὶ κηρυχθήσεται τοῦτο τὸ εὐαγγέλιον τῆς βασιλείας ἐν ὅλῃ τῇ οἰκουμένῃ εἰς μαρτύριον πᾶσιν τοῖς ἔθνεσιν, καὶ τότε ἥξει τὸ τέλος.

24:1 And having come out from the temple Jesus was departing, and his disciples came to him to show him the buildings of the temple; 2 but answering back he said to them, "Do you not see all these things? Amen! I am saying to you, a stone shall certainly not be left here on a stone which shall not be cast down." 3 So, while he was sitting on the Mount of Olives the disciples came to him privately saying, "Tell us when these things shall happen, and what [will be] the sign of your coming and the end of the age?" 4 And answering Jesus said to them, "See to it that no one leads you astray; 5 for many shall come in my name saying; 'I am the Messiah,' and many shall be deceived. 6 So you shall begin to hear of wars and rumors of wars; pay attention, do not be alarmed; for it is necessary for this to happen, but the end is not yet. 7 For nation shall rise against nation and kingdom against kingdom, and there shall be famines and earthquakes from place to place; 8 but all these are the beginning of the birth pangs. 9 Then they will hand you over to tribulation and they will kill you, and you will be hated by all the nations on account of my name. 10 And then many will fall away and they will hand over one another and hate one another; 11 and many false prophets will arise and lead astray many. 12 And because of the abounding of lawlessness the love of many will grow cold. 13 But he who holds on to the end he shall be saved. 14 And this gospel of the kingdom shall be proclaimed in all the world as a testimony to all the nations, and then the end will come."

15 Ὅταν οὖν ἴδητε τὸ βδέλυγμα τῆς ἐρημώσεως τὸ ῥηθὲν διὰ Δανιὴλ τοῦ προφήτου ἑστὸς ἐν τόπῳ ἁγίῳ, ὁ ἀναγινώσκων νοείτω, 16 τότε οἱ ἐν τῇ Ἰουδαίᾳ φευγέτωσαν ἐπὶ τὰ ὄρη, 17 ὁ ἐπὶ τοῦ δώματος μὴ καταβάτω ἆραι τὰ ἐκ τῆς οἰκίας αὐτοῦ, 18 καὶ ὁ ἐν τῷ ἀγρῷ μὴ ἐπιστρεψάτω ὀπίσω ἆραι τὸ ἱμάτιον αὐτοῦ. 19 οὐαὶ δὲ ταῖς ἐν γαστρὶ ἐχούσαις καὶ ταῖς θηλαζούσαις ἐν ἐκείναις ταῖς ἡμέραις. 20 προσεύχεσθε δὲ ἵνα μὴ γένηται ἡ φυγὴ ὑμῶν χειμῶνος μηδὲ σαββάτῳ· 21 ἔσται γὰρ τότε θλῖψις μεγάλη οἵα οὐ γέγονεν ἀπ᾽ ἀρχῆς κόσμου ἕως τοῦ νῦν οὐδ᾽ οὐ μὴ γένηται. 22 καὶ εἰ μὴ ἐκολοβώθησαν αἱ ἡμέραι ἐκεῖναι, οὐκ ἂν ἐσώθη πᾶσα σάρξ· διὰ δὲ τοὺς ἐκλεκτοὺς κολοβωθήσονται αἱ ἡμέραι ἐκεῖναι. 23 τότε ἐάν τις ὑμῖν εἴπῃ· Ἰδοὺ ὧδε ὁ χριστός, ἤ· Ὧδε, μὴ πιστεύσητε· 24 ἐγερθήσονται γὰρ ψευδόχριστοι καὶ ψευδοπροφῆται, καὶ δώσουσιν σημεῖα μεγάλα καὶ τέρατα ὥστε πλανῆσαι εἰ δυνατὸν καὶ τοὺς ἐκλεκτούς· 25 ἰδοὺ προείρηκα ὑμῖν. 26 ἐὰν οὖν εἴπωσιν ὑμῖν· Ἰδοὺ ἐν τῇ ἐρήμῳ ἐστίν, μὴ ἐξέλθητε· Ἰδοὺ ἐν τοῖς ταμείοις, μὴ πιστεύσητε· 27 ὥσπερ γὰρ ἡ ἀστραπὴ ἐξέρχεται ἀπὸ ἀνατολῶν καὶ φαίνεται ἕως δυσμῶν, οὕτως ἔσται ἡ παρουσία τοῦ υἱοῦ τοῦ ἀνθρώπου· 28 ὅπου ἐὰν ᾖ τὸ πτῶμα, ἐκεῖ συναχθήσονται οἱ ἀετοί. 29 Εὐθέως δὲ μετὰ τὴν θλῖψιν τῶν ἡμερῶν ἐκείνων ὁ ἥλιος σκοτισθήσεται, καὶ ἡ σελήνη οὐ δώσει τὸ φέγγος αὐτῆς, καὶ οἱ ἀστέρες πεσοῦνται ἀπὸ τοῦ οὐρανοῦ, καὶ αἱ δυνάμεις τῶν οὐρανῶν σαλευθήσονται. 30 καὶ τότε φανήσεται τὸ σημεῖον τοῦ υἱοῦ τοῦ ἀνθρώπου ἐν τῷ οὐρανῷ, καὶ τότε κόψονται πᾶσαι αἱ φυλαὶ τῆς γῆς καὶ ὄψονται τὸν υἱὸν τοῦ ἀνθρώπου ἐρχόμενον ἐπὶ τῶν νεφελῶν τοῦ οὐρανοῦ μετὰ δυνάμεως καὶ δόξης πολλῆς· 31 καὶ ἀποστελεῖ τοὺς ἀγγέλους αὐτοῦ μετὰ σάλπιγγος μεγάλης, καὶ ἐπισυνάξουσιν τοὺς ἐκλεκτοὺς αὐτοῦ ἐκ τῶν τεσσάρων ἀνέμων ἀπ᾽ ἄκρων οὐρανῶν ἕως τῶν ἄκρων αὐτῶν.

15 "Now when you see the abomination of desolation which was spoken of through Daniel the prophet standing in the holy place, let the reader understand, 16 then let those in Judea flee to the mountains, 17 let the one who is on a rooftop not go down to get the things from his house, 18 and let the one who is in the field not turn back to get his coat. 19 Moreover, woe to those who are pregnant and those who are nursing in those days. 20 So pray in order that your flight might not happen in winter nor the Sabbath; 21 for then there shall be great tribulation such as there has not been from the beginning of the world until now and shall not come to be. 22 And if those days were not shortened, no flesh would be saved; but because of the elect those days will be shortened. 23 Then if someone says to you, 'Behold here is the Messiah, or here,' do not believe [it]; 24 for false Messiahs and false prophets shall arise, and they will give great signs and wonders so as to lead astray if possible even the elect; 25 behold I have told you beforehand. 26 If then they say to you, 'Behold he is in the wilderness,' do not go out; 'Behold in the inner rooms,' do not believe [it]; 27 for just as lightning comes out from the East and shines as far as the West, so shall the coming of the Son of Man be; 28 wherever the corpse is, there the vultures will be gathering. 29 But immediately after the tribulation in those days the sun shall be darkened, and the moon shall not give its light, and the stars shall fall from the sky, and the powers of the heavens shall be shaken. 30 And then the sign of the Son of Man shall appear in the sky, and then all the tribes of the land shall mourn and they shall see the Son of Man coming on the clouds of heaven with great power and glory; 31 and he will send his angels with a great trumpet, and they will gather together his elect from the four winds from one end of the heavens to the other."

Matthew 24:32-51

32 Ἀπὸ δὲ τῆς συκῆς μάθετε τὴν παραβολήν· ὅταν ἤδη ὁ κλάδος αὐτῆς γένηται ἁπαλὸς καὶ τὰ φύλλα ἐκφύῃ, γινώσκετε ὅτι ἐγγὺς τὸ θέρος· 33 οὕτως καὶ ὑμεῖς, ὅταν ἴδητε πάντα ταῦτα, γινώσκετε ὅτι ἐγγύς ἐστιν ἐπὶ θύραις. 34 ἀμὴν λέγω ὑμῖν ὅτι οὐ μὴ παρέλθῃ ἡ γενεὰ αὕτη ἕως ἂν πάντα ταῦτα γένηται. 35 ὁ οὐρανὸς καὶ ἡ γῆ παρελεύσεται, οἱ δὲ λόγοι μου οὐ μὴ παρέλθωσιν. 36 Περὶ δὲ τῆς ἡμέρας ἐκείνης καὶ ὥρας οὐδεὶς οἶδεν, οὐδὲ οἱ ἄγγελοι τῶν οὐρανῶν οὐδὲ ὁ υἱός, εἰ μὴ ὁ πατὴρ μόνος. 37 ὥσπερ γὰρ αἱ ἡμέραι τοῦ Νῶε, οὕτως ἔσται ἡ παρουσία τοῦ υἱοῦ τοῦ ἀνθρώπου· 38 ὡς γὰρ ἦσαν ἐν ταῖς ἡμέραις ταῖς πρὸ τοῦ κατακλυσμοῦ τρώγοντες καὶ πίνοντες, γαμοῦντες καὶ γαμίζοντες, ἄχρι ἧς ἡμέρας εἰσῆλθεν Νῶε εἰς τὴν κιβωτόν, 39 καὶ οὐκ ἔγνωσαν ἕως ἦλθεν ὁ κατακλυσμὸς καὶ ἦρεν ἅπαντας, οὕτως ἔσται καὶ ἡ παρουσία τοῦ υἱοῦ τοῦ ἀνθρώπου. 40 τότε δύο ἔσονται ἐν τῷ ἀγρῷ, εἷς παραλαμβάνεται καὶ εἷς ἀφίεται· 41 δύο ἀλήθουσαι ἐν τῷ μύλῳ, μία παραλαμβάνεται καὶ μία ἀφίεται. 42 γρηγορεῖτε οὖν, ὅτι οὐκ οἴδατε ποίᾳ ἡμέρᾳ ὁ κύριος ὑμῶν ἔρχεται. 43 ἐκεῖνο δὲ γινώσκετε ὅτι εἰ ᾔδει ὁ οἰκοδεσπότης ποίᾳ φυλακῇ ὁ κλέπτης ἔρχεται, ἐγρηγόρησεν ἂν καὶ οὐκ ἂν εἴασεν διορυχθῆναι τὴν οἰκίαν αὐτοῦ. 44 διὰ τοῦτο καὶ ὑμεῖς γίνεσθε ἕτοιμοι, ὅτι ᾗ οὐ δοκεῖτε ὥρᾳ ὁ υἱὸς τοῦ ἀνθρώπου ἔρχεται. 45 Τίς ἄρα ἐστὶν ὁ πιστὸς δοῦλος καὶ φρόνιμος ὃν κατέστησεν ὁ κύριος ἐπὶ τῆς οἰκετείας αὐτοῦ τοῦ δοῦναι αὐτοῖς τὴν τροφὴν ἐν καιρῷ; 46 μακάριος ὁ δοῦλος ἐκεῖνος ὃν ἐλθὼν ὁ κύριος αὐτοῦ εὑρήσει οὕτως ποιοῦντα· 47 ἀμὴν λέγω ὑμῖν ὅτι ἐπὶ πᾶσιν τοῖς ὑπάρχουσιν αὐτοῦ καταστήσει αὐτόν. 48 ἐὰν δὲ εἴπῃ ὁ κακὸς δοῦλος ἐκεῖνος ἐν τῇ καρδίᾳ αὐτοῦ· Χρονίζει μου ὁ κύριος, 49 καὶ ἄρξηται τύπτειν τοὺς συνδούλους αὐτοῦ, ἐσθίῃ δὲ καὶ πίνῃ μετὰ τῶν μεθυόντων, 50 ἥξει ὁ κύριος τοῦ δούλου ἐκείνου ἐν ἡμέρᾳ ᾗ οὐ προσδοκᾷ καὶ ἐν ὥρᾳ ᾗ οὐ γινώσκει, 51 καὶ διχοτομήσει αὐτὸν καὶ τὸ μέρος αὐτοῦ μετὰ τῶν ὑποκριτῶν θήσει· ἐκεῖ ἔσται ὁ κλαυθμὸς καὶ ὁ βρυγμὸς τῶν ὀδόντων.

32 "But from the fig tree parable learn this; now when its branch becomes tender and puts out its leaves, you know that summer is near; 33 so also with you, when you see all these things, you know that it is near, at the gates. 34 Amen! I am saying to you that this generation will certainly not pass away until all these things happen. 35 Heaven and earth shall pass away, but my words shall certainly not pass away. 36 But concerning that day and hour no one knows, neither the angels of the heavens nor the son, except the Father alone. 37 For just as the days of Noah [were], so the coming of the Son of Man shall be; 38 for as they were in those days before the flood, eating and drinking, marrying and giving in marriage, until the day Noah entered into the ark, 39 and they did not know until the flood came and took them all away, so shall the coming of the Son of Man be also. 40 Then two men shall be in a field, one is taken and one left; 41 two women are grinding at the mill, one is taken and one is left. 42 Be alert then, because you do not know on which day your Lord is coming. 43 But you know this, that if the householder had known at which watch the thief is coming, he would have kept watch and not allowed his house to be burglarized. 44 Because of this you also must be ready, for the Son of Man comes at an hour you do not expect. 45 Who then is the faithful and wise servant whom the master puts in charge of his household of servants to give them food at the proper time? 46 Blessed is that servant whom his master will find so doing when he comes. 47 Amen! I am saying to you that over everything he has he shall be put in charge. 48 But if that wicked servant said in his heart, 'My master is delayed,' 49 and began to beat his fellow servants, moreover he ate and drank with the drunkards, 50 the master of that servant will come on a day he does not expect and at an hour he does not know, 51 and he will cut him in two and will assign him a place with the hypocrites; in that place there will be weeping and gnashing of teeth."

Matthew 25:1-18

Κεφ. ΚΕ΄

25:1 Τότε ὁμοιωθήσεται ἡ βασιλεία τῶν οὐρανῶν δέκα παρθένοις, αἵτινες λαβοῦσαι τὰς λαμπάδας ἑαυτῶν ἐξῆλθον εἰς ὑπάντησιν τοῦ νυμφίου. **2** πέντε δὲ ἐξ αὐτῶν ἦσαν μωραὶ καὶ πέντε φρόνιμοι. **3** αἱ γὰρ μωραὶ λαβοῦσαι τὰς λαμπάδας αὐτῶν οὐκ ἔλαβον μεθ᾽ ἑαυτῶν ἔλαιον· **4** αἱ δὲ φρόνιμοι ἔλαβον ἔλαιον ἐν τοῖς ἀγγείοις μετὰ τῶν λαμπάδων ἑαυτῶν.

5 χρονίζοντος δὲ τοῦ νυμφίου ἐνύσταξαν πᾶσαι καὶ ἐκάθευδον. **6** μέσης δὲ νυκτὸς κραυγὴ γέγονεν· Ἰδοὺ ὁ νυμφίος, ἐξέρχεσθε εἰς ἀπάντησιν αὐτοῦ. **7** τότε ἠγέρθησαν πᾶσαι αἱ παρθένοι ἐκεῖναι καὶ ἐκόσμησαν τὰς λαμπάδας ἑαυτῶν. **8** αἱ δὲ μωραὶ ταῖς φρονίμοις εἶπαν· Δότε ἡμῖν ἐκ τοῦ ἐλαίου ὑμῶν, ὅτι αἱ λαμπάδες ἡμῶν σβέννυνται. **9** ἀπεκρίθησαν δὲ αἱ φρόνιμοι λέγουσαι· Μήποτε οὐ μὴ ἀρκέσῃ ἡμῖν καὶ ὑμῖν· πορεύεσθε μᾶλλον πρὸς τοὺς πωλοῦντας καὶ ἀγοράσατε ἑαυταῖς. **10** ἀπερχομένων δὲ αὐτῶν ἀγοράσαι ἦλθεν ὁ νυμφίος, καὶ αἱ ἕτοιμοι εἰσῆλθον μετ᾽ αὐτοῦ εἰς τοὺς γάμους, καὶ ἐκλείσθη ἡ θύρα. **11** ὕστερον δὲ ἔρχονται καὶ αἱ λοιπαὶ παρθένοι λέγουσαι· Κύριε κύριε, ἄνοιξον ἡμῖν· **12** ὁ δὲ ἀποκριθεὶς εἶπεν· Ἀμὴν λέγω ὑμῖν, οὐκ οἶδα ὑμᾶς. **13** γρηγορεῖτε οὖν, ὅτι οὐκ οἴδατε τὴν ἡμέραν οὐδὲ τὴν ὥραν. **14** Ὥσπερ γὰρ ἄνθρωπος ἀποδημῶν ἐκάλεσεν τοὺς ἰδίους δούλους καὶ παρέδωκεν αὐτοῖς τὰ ὑπάρχοντα αὐτοῦ, **15** καὶ ᾧ μὲν ἔδωκεν πέντε τάλαντα ᾧ δὲ δύο ᾧ δὲ ἕν, ἑκάστῳ κατὰ τὴν ἰδίαν δύναμιν, καὶ ἀπεδήμησεν. εὐθέως **16** πορευθεὶς ὁ τὰ πέντε τάλαντα λαβὼν ἠργάσατο ἐν αὐτοῖς καὶ ἐκέρδησεν ἄλλα πέντε· **17** ὡσαύτως ὁ τὰ δύο ἐκέρδησεν ἄλλα δύο· **18** ὁ δὲ τὸ ἓν λαβὼν ἀπελθὼν ὤρυξεν γῆν καὶ ἔκρυψεν τὸ ἀργύριον τοῦ κυρίου αὐτοῦ.

25:1 "Then the Kingdom of the Heavens shall be like ten virgins, who taking their lamps went out to meet the bridegroom. [2] Now five of them were foolish and five wise. [3] For the five foolish ones, having taken their lamps, did not bring with them oil; [4] but the wise ones brought oil in the flasks with their lamps. [5] So, when the bridegroom delayed in coming all became drowsy and were sleeping. [6] But in the middle of the night a cry was made, 'Behold the bridegroom, come out to meet him!' [7] Then all those virgins were awakened and they put in order their lamps. [8] But the foolish ones said, 'Give us of your oil, for our lamps are going out.' [9] Now the wise ones answered saying, 'Certainly there would not be enough for us and you; go rather to those who sell and buy [some] for yourselves.' [10] But while they were going out to buy the bridegroom came, and the prepared ones entered with him into the wedding feast, and the door was shut. [11] So later the other virgins also came saying, 'Lord Lord, open up for us;' [12] but answering back he said, 'Amen! I am saying to you, I do not know you.' [13] Then keep watch, for you do not know the day nor the hour. [14] For just as a man leaving on a journey called his own servants and entrusted to them his possessions, [15] and one he gave five talents but to another two but to another one, to each according to his own ability, and he left on a journey. Immediately, [16] going, the one who received the five talents traded with them and gained another five; [17] similarly the one with two gained another two; [18] but the one who received one, departing, dug in the ground and hid the silver of his master."

Matthew 25:19-30

19 μετὰ δὲ πολὺν χρόνον ἔρχεται ὁ κύριος τῶν δούλων ἐκείνων καὶ συναίρει λόγον μετ' αὐτῶν 20 καὶ προσελθὼν ὁ τὰ πέντε τάλαντα λαβὼν προσήνεγκεν ἄλλα πέντε τάλαντα λέγων·

Κύριε, πέντε τάλαντά μοι παρέδωκας· ἴδε ἄλλα πέντε τάλαντα ἐκέρδησα.

21 ἔφη αὐτῷ ὁ κύριος αὐτοῦ·

Εὖ, δοῦλε ἀγαθὲ καὶ πιστέ, ἐπὶ ὀλίγα ἦς πιστός, ἐπὶ πολλῶν σε καταστήσω· εἴσελθε εἰς τὴν χαρὰν τοῦ κυρίου σου.

22 προσελθὼν δὲ καὶ ὁ τὰ δύο τάλαντα εἶπεν·

Κύριε, δύο τάλαντά μοι παρέδωκας· ἴδε ἄλλα δύο τάλαντα ἐκέρδησα.

23 ἔφη αὐτῷ ὁ κύριος αὐτοῦ·

Εὖ, δοῦλε ἀγαθὲ καὶ πιστέ, ἐπὶ ὀλίγα ἦς πιστός, ἐπὶ πολλῶν σε καταστήσω· εἴσελθε εἰς τὴν χαρὰν τοῦ κυρίου σου.

24 προσελθὼν δὲ καὶ ὁ τὸ ἓν τάλαντον εἰληφὼς εἶπεν·

Κύριε, ἔγνων σε ὅτι σκληρὸς εἶ ἄνθρωπος, θερίζων ὅπου οὐκ ἔσπειρας καὶ συνάγων ὅθεν οὐ διεσκόρπισας· 25 καὶ φοβηθεὶς ἀπελθὼν ἔκρυψα τὸ τάλαντόν σου ἐν τῇ γῇ· ἴδε ἔχεις τὸ σόν.

26 ἀποκριθεὶς δὲ ὁ κύριος αὐτοῦ εἶπεν αὐτῷ·

Πονηρὲ δοῦλε καὶ ὀκνηρέ, ᾔδεις ὅτι θερίζω ὅπου οὐκ ἔσπειρα καὶ συνάγω ὅθεν οὐ διεσκόρπισα; 27 ἔδει σε οὖν βαλεῖν τὰ ἀργύριά μου τοῖς τραπεζίταις, καὶ ἐλθὼν ἐγὼ ἐκομισάμην ἂν τὸ ἐμὸν σὺν τόκῳ. 28 ἄρατε οὖν ἀπ' αὐτοῦ τὸ τάλαντον καὶ δότε τῷ ἔχοντι τὰ δέκα τάλαντα· 29 τῷ γὰρ ἔχοντι παντὶ δοθήσεται καὶ περισσευθήσεται· τοῦ δὲ μὴ ἔχοντος καὶ ὃ ἔχει ἀρθήσεται ἀπ' αὐτοῦ. 30 καὶ τὸν ἀχρεῖον δοῦλον ἐκβάλετε εἰς τὸ σκότος τὸ ἐξώτερον· ἐκεῖ ἔσται ὁ κλαυθμὸς καὶ ὁ βρυγμὸς τῶν ὀδόντων.

19 "So after a long time the master of those servants comes and settles accounts with them 20 and, approaching, the one who received five talents brought another five talents saying, 'Master, you handed me five talents; behold I gained another five talents.' 21 His master said to him, 'Well done, good and faithful servant, over a few things you were faithful, over many things I shall put you in charge; enter into the joy of your master.' 22 Now, approaching, the one with two talents said, 'Master, you handed me two talents; behold I gained another two talents.' 23 His master said to him, 'Well done good and faithful servant, over a few things you were faithful, over many things I shall put you in charge; enter into the joy of your master.' 24 So, also approaching, the one who had received one talent said, 'Master, I knew that you are a hard man, reaping where you did not sow and gathering from where you did not scatter; 25 and being afraid and leaving I hid your talent in the ground; behold you have that which is yours.' 26 But answering back his master said to him, 'Evil and lazy servant, did you know that I reap where I did not sow and gather? 27 Then it was necessary for you to put my money with the bankers, so when I came I would have recovered that which is mine with interest. 28 Take then from him the talent and give it to the one who has ten talents; 29 for to the one who has much shall be given and he shall have an abundance; but the one who does not have even that which he has shall be taken away from him. 30 And cast out the useless servant into the outer darkness; in that place there shall be weeping and gnashing of teeth.'"

Matthew 25:31-43

31 Ὅταν δὲ ἔλθῃ ὁ υἱὸς τοῦ ἀνθρώπου ἐν τῇ δόξῃ αὐτοῦ καὶ πάντες οἱ ἄγγελοι μετ' αὐτοῦ, τότε καθίσει ἐπὶ θρόνου δόξης αὐτοῦ· 32 καὶ συναχθήσονται ἔμπροσθεν αὐτοῦ πάντα τὰ ἔθνη, καὶ ἀφορίσει αὐτοὺς ἀπ' ἀλλήλων, ὥσπερ ὁ ποιμὴν ἀφορίζει τὰ πρόβατα ἀπὸ τῶν ἐρίφων, 33 καὶ στήσει τὰ μὲν πρόβατα ἐκ δεξιῶν αὐτοῦ τὰ δὲ ἐρίφια ἐξ εὐωνύμων. 34 τότε ἐρεῖ ὁ βασιλεὺς τοῖς ἐκ δεξιῶν αὐτοῦ· Δεῦτε, οἱ εὐλογημένοι τοῦ πατρός μου, κληρονομήσατε τὴν ἡτοιμασμένην ὑμῖν βασιλείαν ἀπὸ καταβολῆς κόσμου. 35 ἐπείνασα γὰρ καὶ ἐδώκατέ μοι φαγεῖν, ἐδίψησα καὶ ἐποτίσατέ με, ξένος ἤμην καὶ συνηγάγετέ με, 36 γυμνὸς καὶ περιεβάλετέ με, ἠσθένησα καὶ ἐπεσκέψασθέ με, ἐν φυλακῇ ἤμην καὶ ἤλθατε πρός με. 37 τότε ἀποκριθήσονται αὐτῷ οἱ δίκαιοι λέγοντες· Κύριε, πότε σε εἴδομεν πεινῶντα καὶ ἐθρέψαμεν, ἢ διψῶντα καὶ ἐποτίσαμεν; 38 πότε δέ σε εἴδομεν ξένον καὶ συνηγάγομεν, ἢ γυμνὸν καὶ περιεβάλομεν; 39 πότε δέ σε εἴδομεν ἀσθενοῦντα ἢ ἐν φυλακῇ καὶ ἤλθομεν πρός σε; 40 καὶ ἀποκριθεὶς ὁ βασιλεὺς ἐρεῖ αὐτοῖς· Ἀμὴν λέγω ὑμῖν, ἐφ' ὅσον ἐποιήσατε ἑνὶ τούτων τῶν ἀδελφῶν μου τῶν ἐλαχίστων, ἐμοὶ ἐποιήσατε. 41 τότε ἐρεῖ καὶ τοῖς ἐξ εὐωνύμων· Πορεύεσθε ἀπ' ἐμοῦ οἱ κατηραμένοι εἰς τὸ πῦρ τὸ αἰώνιον τὸ ἡτοιμασμένον τῷ διαβόλῳ καὶ τοῖς ἀγγέλοις αὐτοῦ. 42 ἐπείνασα γὰρ καὶ οὐκ ἐδώκατέ μοι φαγεῖν, ἐδίψησα καὶ οὐκ ἐποτίσατέ με, 43 ξένος ἤμην καὶ οὐ συνηγάγετέ με, γυμνὸς καὶ οὐ περιεβάλετέ με, ἀσθενὴς καὶ ἐν φυλακῇ καὶ οὐκ ἐπεσκέψασθέ με.

31 "So whenever the Son of Man might come in his glory and all his angels with him, then he shall sit upon his throne of glory. 32 And all the nations shall be gathered before him, and he shall separate them from each other, just as the shepherd separates the sheep from the goats, 33 and the sheep he will place at his right but the goats at his left. 34 Then the king shall say to those on his right, 'Come, you who are blessed by my Father, inherit the kingdom that was prepared for you from the foundation of the world. 35 For I was hungry and you gave me to eat, I was thirsty and you gave me a drink, I was a stranger and you invited me as a guest, 36 I was naked and you clothed me, I was sick and you cared for me, I was in prison and you came to me.' 37 Then the righteous ones shall answer him back saying, 'Lord, when did we see you hungering and feed you, or thirsting and give you a drink? 38 Additionally, when did we see you a stranger and welcome you as a guest, or naked and clothe you? 39 Moreover, when did we see you sick or in prison and come to you?' 40 And answering back the king shall say to them, 'Amen! I am saying to you, the extent of what you did to one of the least of these brothers of mine, you did to me.' 41 Then he shall also say to those on the left, 'Depart from me you who are cursed to the eternal fire which is prepared for the devil and his angels. 42 For I was hungry and you did not give me to eat, I was thirsty and you did not give a drink to me, 43 I was a stranger and you did not invite me as a guest, and I was naked and you did not clothe me, weak and in prison and you did not visit me.'"

Matthew 25:44-26:5

[44] "Then they shall also reply saying, 'Lord, when did we see you hungering or thirsting or a stranger or naked or weak or in prison and did not help you?' [45] Then he shall answer them back saying, 'Amen! I am saying to you, the extent of what you did not do to one of the least of these, neither did you do unto me. [46] And these ones shall go away into eternal punishment, but the righteous into eternal life.'" 26:1 And it happened when Jesus finished all these words, he said to his disciples, [2] "You know that after two days Passover is coming, and the Son of Man is handed over to be crucified." [3] Then the high priests and the elders of the people were gathered together in the court of the high priest who is called Caiaphas, [4] and they plotted in order that they might grasp Jesus by deceit and kill [him]; [5] but they were saying, "Not during the festival, so that there may not be a riot among the people."

Matthew 26:6-16

⁶ And when Jesus was in Bethany in the house of Simon the skin diseased, ⁷ a woman came to him having an alabaster jar of expensive ointment and poured it over his head as he reclined. ⁸ But seeing [this] the disciples were indignant saying, "To what end this waste? ⁹ For this was able to be sold for a lot and given to the poor." ¹⁰ But knowing [this] Jesus said to them, "Why do you give trouble to this woman? For she has done a good thing to me. ¹¹ For you always have the poor with you, but me you do not always have; ¹² for when she poured this ointment on my body she prepared me for burial. ¹³ Amen I am saying to you, whenever this good news is proclaimed in all the world, what she did shall also be spoken of in memory of her." ¹⁴ Then one of the twelve, who is called Judas Iscariot, walking to the high priests ¹⁵ said, "What are you willing to give me and I will hand him over to you?" So they weighed out to him thirty pieces of silver. ¹⁶ And from that time he was seeking a favorable time so that he might hand him over.

Matthew 26:17-26

[17] So on the first day of Unleavened Bread the disciples came to Jesus saying, "Where do you want us to prepare for you to eat the Passover?" [18] So he said, "Go into the city to a certain person and say to him, 'The teacher says;' 'My time is near; with you I keep the Passover with my disciples.'" [19] And the disciples did as Jesus directed them, and they prepared the Passover. [20] So when evening came he was reclining with the twelve disciples [21] and while eating with them he said, "Amen I am saying to you that one of you shall betray me." [22] And greatly grieved they each began to say to him, "Surely not I, Lord?" [23] So answering back he said, "The one who dipped the hand with me in the bowl he will betray me; [24] the Son of Man departs just as it has been written about him, but woe to that man through whom the Son of Man is handed over; it would have been better for that man if he was not born." [25] Now answering back Judas his betrayer said, "Surely not I, Rabbi?" He says to him, "You said [it]." [26] Now as they were eating, Jesus, having taken and having given a blessing of the bread, having broken and given [it] to the disciples said;

Matthew 26:26-34

"Take, eat, this is my body." ²⁷ And taking a cup and giving thanks he gave [it] to them saying, "Drink out of it all of you, ²⁸ for this is my blood of the covenant which is being poured out for many for the forgiveness of sins; ²⁹ but I am saying to you, from now on I will not drink of this fruit of the vine until that day when I drink it anew with you in the kingdom of my Father." ³⁰ And after singing a hymn they went out onto the Mount of Olives. ³¹ Then Jesus says to them, "All of you will fall away because of me this night, for it has been written, 'I will strike the shepherd, and the sheep of the flock will be scattered;' ³² but after I have been raised I shall go before you into the Galilee." ³³ So answering back Peter said to him, "If everyone shall fall away because of you, I shall never fall away." ³⁴ Jesus said to him, "Amen! I am saying to you that on this night before a rooster crows you will deny me three times."

Matthew 26:35-42

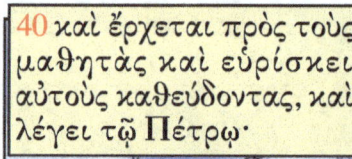

Matthew 26:43-53

43 καὶ ἐλθὼν πάλιν εὗρεν αὐτοὺς καθεύδοντας, ἦσαν γὰρ αὐτῶν οἱ ὀφθαλμοὶ βεβαρημένοι. 44 καὶ ἀφεὶς αὐτοὺς πάλιν ἀπελθὼν προσηύξατο ἐκ τρίτου τὸν αὐτὸν λόγον εἰπὼν πάλιν. 45 τότε ἔρχεται πρὸς τοὺς μαθητὰς καὶ λέγει αὐτοῖς·

Καθεύδετε τὸ λοιπὸν καὶ ἀναπαύεσθε· ἰδοὺ ἤγγικεν ἡ ὥρα καὶ ὁ υἱὸς τοῦ ἀνθρώπου παραδίδοται εἰς χεῖρας ἁμαρτωλῶν. 46 ἐγείρεσθε ἄγωμεν· ἰδοὺ ἤγγικεν ὁ παραδιδούς με.

47 Καὶ ἔτι αὐτοῦ λαλοῦντος ἰδοὺ Ἰούδας εἷς τῶν δώδεκα ἦλθεν καὶ μετ' αὐτοῦ ὄχλος πολὺς μετὰ μαχαιρῶν καὶ ξύλων ἀπὸ τῶν ἀρχιερέων καὶ πρεσβυτέρων τοῦ λαοῦ. 48 ὁ δὲ παραδιδοὺς αὐτὸν ἔδωκεν αὐτοῖς σημεῖον λέγων·

Ὃν ἂν φιλήσω αὐτός ἐστιν· κρατήσατε αὐτόν.

49 καὶ εὐθέως προσελθὼν τῷ Ἰησοῦ εἶπεν·

Χαῖρε, ῥαββί·

καὶ κατεφίλησεν αὐτόν.

50 ὁ δὲ Ἰησοῦς εἶπεν αὐτῷ·

Ἑταῖρε, ἐφ' ὃ πάρει.

τότε προσελθόντες ἐπέβαλον τὰς χεῖρας ἐπὶ τὸν Ἰησοῦν καὶ ἐκράτησαν αὐτόν.

51 καὶ ἰδοὺ εἷς τῶν μετὰ Ἰησοῦ ἐκτείνας τὴν χεῖρα ἀπέσπασεν τὴν μάχαιραν αὐτοῦ

καὶ πατάξας τὸν δοῦλον τοῦ ἀρχιερέως ἀφεῖλεν αὐτοῦ τὸ ὠτίον.

52 τότε λέγει αὐτῷ ὁ Ἰησοῦς·

Ἀπόστρεψον τὴν μάχαιράν σου εἰς τὸν τόπον αὐτῆς, πάντες γὰρ οἱ λαβόντες μάχαιραν ἐν μαχαίρῃ ἀπολοῦνται· 53 ἢ δοκεῖς ὅτι οὐ δύναμαι παρακαλέσαι τὸν πατέρα μου, καὶ παραστήσει μοι ἄρτι πλείω δώδεκα λεγιῶνας ἀγγέλων;

43 And coming, again he found them sleeping for their eyes were heavy. 44 And having left them, again going away, he prayed a third time saying again the same thing. 45 Then he comes to the disciples and says to them, "Are you still sleeping and resting; behold the hour has come and the Son of Man is being handed over into the hands of sinners. 46 Get up! Let us go; behold the one betraying me has come." 47 And while he was still speaking behold Judas one of the twelve came and with him a great crowd with swords and clubs from the high priests and elders of the people. 48 Now the one betraying him gave them a sign saying, "Whomever I kiss it is he; seize him!" 49 And immediately after coming to Jesus he said, "Greetings, Rabbi;" and he kissed him. 50 Now Jesus said to him, "Friend, why are you here?" Then coming they laid their hands on Jesus and seized him. 51 And behold one of those with Jesus, stretching out [his] hand, drew his sword and striking the servant of the high priest he took off his ear. 52 Then Jesus says to him, "Put your sword back in its place, for all who take a sword shall die by a sword; 53 or do you not think that I am able to urge my Father, and he will provide me just now more than twelve legions of angels?"

Matthew 26:54-63

[54] "How then would the Scriptures be fulfilled that in this manner it must happen?" [55] In that hour Jesus said to the crowds, "As against a robber you came with swords and clubs to apprehend me? Daily in the temple I was sitting teaching and you did not seize me. [56] But all this has happened in order to fulfill the writings of the prophets." Then all the disciples, leaving him, fled. [57] So those seizing Jesus led him to Caiaphas the high priest, where the scribes and the elders had gathered together. [58] But Peter was following him from afar as far as the courtyard of the high priest, and after entering in he was sitting within with the servants to see the outcome. [59] But the high priests and the Sanhedrin were all seeking a false witness against Jesus in order that they might kill him, [60] and they did not find many false witnesses coming forward. But finally, coming forward, two [61] said, "This man said; 'I am able to destroy the temple of God and in three days build [it].'" [62] And standing up the high priest said to him, "Do you answer nothing about what these ones are testifying against you?" [63] But Jesus kept silent.

Matthew 26:63-71

And the high priest said to him, "I adjure you according to the living God that you say if you are the Messiah the Son of God." ⁶⁴ Jesus says to him, "You yourself said [it]; however, I am saying to you, from now on you will see the Son of Man sitting at the right hand of power, and coming upon the clouds of heaven." ⁶⁵ Then the high priest tore his clothes saying, "He blasphemed! What need do we still have of witnesses? Behold, now you heard the blasphemy! ⁶⁶ How does it seem to you?" So answering they said, "He deserves death!" ⁶⁷ Then they spat in his face and struck him, moreover others slapped [him] ⁶⁸ saying, "Prophesy for us, Messiah, who is the one who struck you?" ⁶⁹ But Peter was sitting outside in the courtyard; and a lone maidservant came to him saying, "You also were with Jesus of Galilee;" ⁷⁰ but he denied in front of everyone saying, "I do not know what you are saying." ⁷¹ But when he went toward the gate another one saw him and says to those who are there, "This one was with Jesus of Nazareth;"

Matthew 26:72-27:4

[72] and again he denied [it] with an oath [saying] this; "I do not know the man." [73] But after a little while, approaching, those standing near said to Peter, "Truly you yourself are also one of them, for even your speech makes you noticeable;" [74] then he began to curse and swear this; "I do not know the man!" And immediately a rooster crowed. [75] And Peter remembered the saying of Jesus who had said this; "Before a rooster crows, three times you will deny me," and after going outside he wept bitterly. 27:1 Now when morning came all the high priests and elders of the people took council against Jesus so as to put him to death; [2] and binding him they led him away and handed him over to Pilate the governor. [3] Then Judas who handed him over, seeing that he was condemned, being remorseful returned the thirty pieces of silver to the high priests and elders [4] saying, "I sinned handing over innocent blood."

But they said, "What is this to us? You see to it." ⁵ And having thrown the silver into the temple he left, and after leaving the hanged [himself]. ⁶ So the high priests, after taking the silver, said, "It is not lawful to put these into the treasury, since it is the price of blood;" ⁷ so after taking council they bought with them the Potter's Field as a burial place for strangers. ⁸ Therefore, that field is called Blood Field to this day. ⁹ Then was fulfilled that which was spoken through Jeremiah the prophet saying, ¹⁰ "And they took the thirty pieces of silver, the price of one who had been priced, who some of the sons of Israel priced, and they gave them for the Potter's Field, just as the LORD directed me." ¹¹ So Jesus was put before the governor; and the governor questioned him saying, "Are you the king of the Jews?" But Jesus said, "You are saying [it]." ¹² And as he was being accused by the high priests and elders he did not answer anything. ¹³ Then Pilate says to him, "Do you not hear how many things they are testifying against you?" ¹⁴ And he did not answer him not even one word, so as [to cause] the governor to marvel greatly. ¹⁵ Now at each festival the governor had been accustomed to release one prisoner to the crowd who they were wanting. ¹⁶ Now then, they were holding a notorious prisoner named Jesus Barabbas. ¹⁷ Then after they had been gathered Pilate said to them, "Who do you want me to release to you, Jesus Barabbas or Jesus who is called the Messiah?" ¹⁸ For he had known that because of envy they handed him over.

Matthew 27:19-25

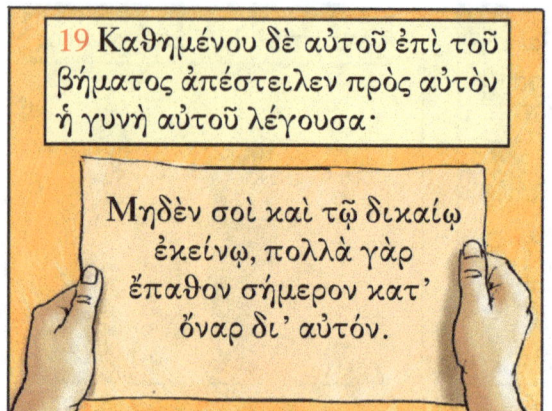

[19] So, while he was sitting upon the judgment seat his wife sent [word] to him saying, "You also have nothing to do with that man, for I suffered much today in a dream because of him." [20] But the high priests and the elders persuaded the crowds to ask for Barabbas but destroy Jesus. [21] Now answering back the governor said to them, "Which of these two do you want me to release to you?" So they said, "Barabbas." [22] Pilate says to them, "What then should I do to Jesus called the Messiah?" They all say, "Let him be crucified!" [23] But he said, "Why? For what evil did he do?" But they kept crying out louder saying, "Let him be crucified!" [24] Now Pilate, having seen that he is accomplishing nothing but rather a riot is occurring, taking water he washed hands before the crowd saying, "I am innocent of this blood; You will see [to it]." [25] And answering back all the people said, "His blood [be] on us and our children."

26 τότε ἀπέλυσεν αὐτοῖς τὸν Βαραββᾶν, τὸν δὲ Ἰησοῦν φραγελλώσας παρέδωκεν ἵνα σταυρωθῇ.

27 Τότε οἱ στρατιῶται τοῦ ἡγεμόνος παραλαβόντες τὸν Ἰησοῦν εἰς τὸ πραιτώριον συνήγαγον ἐπ' αὐτὸν ὅλην τὴν σπεῖραν. 28 καὶ ἐκδύσαντες αὐτὸν χλαμύδα κοκκίνην περιέθηκαν αὐτῷ, 29 καὶ πλέξαντες στέφανον ἐξ ἀκανθῶν ἐπέθηκαν ἐπὶ τῆς κεφαλῆς αὐτοῦ καὶ κάλαμον ἐν τῇ δεξιᾷ αὐτοῦ, καὶ γονυπετήσαντες ἔμπροσθεν αὐτοῦ ἐνέπαιξαν αὐτῷ λέγοντες·

Χαῖρε, βασιλεῦ τῶν Ἰουδαίων,

30 καὶ ἐμπτύσαντες εἰς αὐτὸν ἔλαβον τὸν κάλαμον καὶ ἔτυπτον εἰς τὴν κεφαλὴν αὐτοῦ. 31 καὶ ὅτε ἐνέπαιξαν αὐτῷ, ἐξέδυσαν αὐτὸν τὴν χλαμύδα καὶ ἐνέδυσαν αὐτὸν τὰ ἱμάτια αὐτοῦ καὶ ἀπήγαγον αὐτὸν εἰς τὸ σταυρῶσαι.

32 Ἐξερχόμενοι δὲ εὗρον ἄνθρωπον Κυρηναῖον ὀνόματι Σίμωνα· τοῦτον ἠγγάρευσαν ἵνα ἄρῃ τὸν σταυρὸν αὐτοῦ.

33 Καὶ ἐλθόντες εἰς τόπον λεγόμενον Γολγοθᾶ, ὅ ἐστιν Κρανίου Τόπος λεγόμενος,

34 ἔδωκαν αὐτῷ πιεῖν οἶνον μετὰ χολῆς μεμιγμένον· καὶ γευσάμενος οὐκ ἠθέλησεν πιεῖν.

[26] Then he released to them Barabbas, but Jesus after being scourged, was handed over in order to be crucified. [27] Then the soldiers of the governor, having taken Jesus into the Praetorium, gathered the whole cohort against him. [28] And having stripped him they placed a scarlet robe on him, [29] and weaving a crown out of thorns they laid [it] upon his head and [placed] a reed stick in his right hand, and kneeling before him they mocked him saying, "Hail, king of the Jews!" [30] And spitting on him they took the reed and kept beating on his head. [31] And when they had mocked him they took off of him the robe and put on him his clothes and led him away to be crucified. [32] Now as they are going out they find a man, a Cyrenian, named Simon; they forced this man into service so that he might carry his cross. [33] And having come to the place called Golgotha, which means "Place of the Skull," [34] they gave to him wine mixed with gall to drink; and after tasting it he did not want to drink.

Matthew 27:35-44

35 Now when they had crucified him they divided up his clothes [by] casting lot, 36 and as they were sitting down they were guarding him there. 37 And they put above his head his written charge, "This is Jesus the king of the Jews." 38 Then two robbers are being crucified with him, one on his right and one on his left. 39 Now those passing by were reviling him shaking their heads 40 and saying, "The one who is destroying the temple and in three days is building it up, save yourself; if you are the Son of God, come down from the cross." 41 Likewise also the high priests, mocking with the scribes and elders, were saying, 42 "Others he saved, himself he is not able to save; he is the king of Israel, now let him come down from the cross and we shall believe in him. 43 He has trusted in God, now deliver him if He wants to, for he said this; 'I am the son of God.'" 44 Moreover, even the robbers who were crucified with him were reproaching him with them.

Matthew 27:45-53

⁴⁵ Ἀπὸ δὲ ἕκτης ὥρας σκότος ἐγένετο ἐπὶ πᾶσαν τὴν γῆν ἕως ὥρας ἐνάτης. ⁴⁶ περὶ δὲ τὴν ἐνάτην ὥραν ἀνεβόησεν ὁ Ἰησοῦς φωνῇ μεγάλῃ λέγων·

Ἠλὶ ἠλὶ λεμὰ σαβαχθάνι;

τοῦτ᾿ ἔστιν· Θεέ μου θεέ μου, ἱνατί με ἐγκατέλιπες;

⁴⁷ τινὲς δὲ τῶν ἐκεῖ ἑστηκότων ἀκούσαντες ἔλεγον ὅτι

Ἠλίαν φωνεῖ οὗτος.

⁴⁸ καὶ εὐθέως δραμὼν εἷς ἐξ αὐτῶν καὶ λαβὼν σπόγγον πλήσας τε ὄξους καὶ περιθεὶς καλάμῳ ἐπότιζεν αὐτόν. ⁴⁹ οἱ δὲ λοιποὶ ἔλεγον·

Ἄφες ἴδωμεν εἰ ἔρχεται Ἠλίας σώσων αὐτόν.

⁵⁰ ὁ δὲ Ἰησοῦς πάλιν κράξας φωνῇ μεγάλῃ ἀφῆκεν τὸ πνεῦμα.

⁵¹ καὶ ἰδοὺ τὸ καταπέτασμα τοῦ ναοῦ ἐσχίσθη ἀπ᾿ ἄνωθεν ἕως κάτω εἰς δύο, καὶ ἡ γῆ ἐσείσθη, καὶ αἱ πέτραι ἐσχίσθησαν, ⁵² καὶ τὰ μνημεῖα ἀνεῴχθησαν καὶ πολλὰ σώματα τῶν κεκοιμημένων ἁγίων ἠγέρθησαν, ⁵³ καὶ ἐξελθόντες ἐκ τῶν μνημείων μετὰ τὴν ἔγερσιν αὐτοῦ εἰσῆλθον εἰς τὴν ἁγίαν πόλιν καὶ ἐνεφανίσθησαν πολλοῖς.

⁴⁵ But from the sixth hour darkness came over the whole land until the ninth hour. ⁴⁶ Now in the ninth hour Jesus cried out with a loud voice saying, "Eli Eli Lema Sabbachthani?" Which means; my God my God, why did you forsake me? ⁴⁷ Now some of those standing there, hearing [this], were saying this; "This man is calling Elijah." ⁴⁸ And immediately one of them, running and taking a sponge, filling it with sour wine, placing it on a reed, was giving it to him to drink. ⁴⁹ But the rest were saying, "Halt! let us see if Elijah comes to save him." ⁵⁰ But Jesus again crying out with a loud voice gave up the spirit. ⁵¹ And behold, the veil of the temple tore from top to bottom into two [pieces], and the earth was shaken, and the rocks were split open, ⁵² and the tombs were opened and many bodies of the holy ones who had fallen asleep were raised, ⁵³ and having come out of the tombs after his resurrection they entered into the holy city and appeared to many.

Matthew 27:54-64

54 Ὁ δὲ ἑκατόνταρχος καὶ οἱ μετ' αὐτοῦ τηροῦντες τὸν Ἰησοῦν ἰδόντες τὸν σεισμὸν καὶ τὰ γενόμενα ἐφοβήθησαν σφόδρα λέγοντες·

Ἀληθῶς θεοῦ υἱὸς ἦν οὗτος.

55 Ἦσαν δὲ ἐκεῖ γυναῖκες πολλαὶ ἀπὸ μακρόθεν θεωροῦσαι, αἵτινες ἠκολούθησαν τῷ Ἰησοῦ ἀπὸ τῆς Γαλιλαίας διακονοῦσαι αὐτῷ· **56** ἐν αἷς ἦν Μαρία ἡ Μαγδαληνὴ καὶ Μαρία ἡ τοῦ Ἰακώβου καὶ Ἰωσὴφ μήτηρ καὶ ἡ μήτηρ τῶν υἱῶν Ζεβεδαίου.

57 Ὀψίας δὲ γενομένης ἦλθεν ἄνθρωπος πλούσιος ἀπὸ Ἁριμαθαίας, τοὔνομα Ἰωσήφ, ὃς καὶ αὐτὸς ἐμαθητεύθη τῷ Ἰησοῦ· **58** οὗτος προσελθὼν τῷ Πιλάτῳ ᾐτήσατο τὸ σῶμα τοῦ Ἰησοῦ. τότε ὁ Πιλᾶτος ἐκέλευσεν ἀποδοθῆναι. **59** καὶ λαβὼν τὸ σῶμα ὁ Ἰωσὴφ ἐνετύλιξεν αὐτὸ σινδόνι καθαρᾷ, **60** καὶ ἔθηκεν αὐτὸ ἐν τῷ καινῷ αὐτοῦ μνημείῳ ὃ ἐλατόμησεν ἐν τῇ πέτρᾳ, καὶ προσκυλίσας λίθον μέγαν τῇ θύρᾳ τοῦ μνημείου ἀπῆλθεν. **61** ἦν δὲ ἐκεῖ Μαριὰμ ἡ Μαγδαληνὴ καὶ ἡ ἄλλη Μαρία καθήμεναι ἀπέναντι τοῦ τάφου.

62 Τῇ δὲ ἐπαύριον, ἥτις ἐστὶν μετὰ τὴν παρασκευήν, συνήχθησαν οἱ ἀρχιερεῖς καὶ οἱ Φαρισαῖοι πρὸς Πιλᾶτον **63** λέγοντες·

Κύριε, ἐμνήσθημεν ὅτι ἐκεῖνος ὁ πλάνος εἶπεν ἔτι ζῶν· Μετὰ τρεῖς ἡμέρας ἐγείρομαι· **64** κέλευσον οὖν ἀσφαλισθῆναι τὸν τάφον ἕως τῆς τρίτης ἡμέρας, μήποτε ἐλθόντες οἱ μαθηταὶ αὐτοῦ κλέψωσιν αὐτὸν καὶ εἴπωσιν τῷ λαῷ· Ἠγέρθη ἀπὸ τῶν νεκρῶν, καὶ ἔσται ἡ ἐσχάτη πλάνη χείρων τῆς πρώτης.

[54] But when the Centurion and those with him guarding Jesus saw the earthquake and the things that happened they became very afraid saying, "Truly this man was God's son." [55] Now there were many women there observing from afar, who followed Jesus from the Galilee ministering to him; [56] among whom were Mary Magdalene and Mary the mother of James and Joseph and the mother of the sons of Zebedee. [57] Now as evening arrived a rich man from Arimethea came, named Joseph, who himself was also a disciple of Jesus; [58] He himself, going to Pilate, asked for the body of Jesus. Then Pilate ordered [it] to be given back. [59] And taking the body Joseph wrapped it in clean linen cloth, [60] and placed it in his own new burial chamber which he had cut in the rock, and having rolled a great stone to the door of the tomb he left. [61] So it was there Mary Magdalene and the other Mary were sitting opposite the grave. [62] Now in the morning, which is after the day of preparation, the high priests and the Pharisees were gathered unto Pilate [63] saying, "Sir, we remembered that while that deceiver was still alive he said, 'After three days I am raised;' [64] order then to make secure the grave until the third day, lest having come his disciples might steal him and say to the people, 'He is raised from the dead,' and the last deception shall be worse than the first."

Matthew 27:65-28:7

⁶⁵ Pilate said to them, "You have a guard; go, make it as secure as you know [how to do]." ⁶⁶ Now going they made secure the grave, sealing the stone [along] with [posting] the guard. 28:1 So, after the Sabbath, at dawn on the first day of the week, Mary Magdalene and the other Mary came to see the grave. ² And behold there was a great earthquake; for an angel of the LORD, descending out of heaven and approaching, rolled away the stone and was sitting upon it. ³ Moreover, his appearance was as lightning and his robe was white as snow. ⁴ But from fear of him the guards trembled and they became as dead men. ⁵ But answering the angel said to the women, "You yourselves do not be afraid, for I know that you are seeking Jesus who was crucified; ⁶ he is not here, for he was raised just as he said; come see the place where he was laid down; ⁷ and going quickly say to his disciples this; 'He was raised from the dead, and behold he is going before you into the Galilee, there you shall see him;' behold I told you."

Matthew 28:8-20

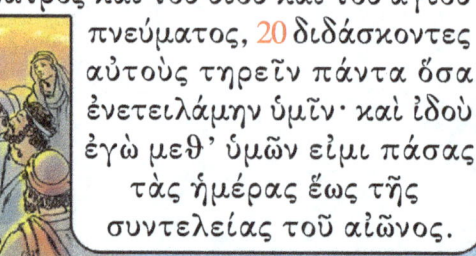
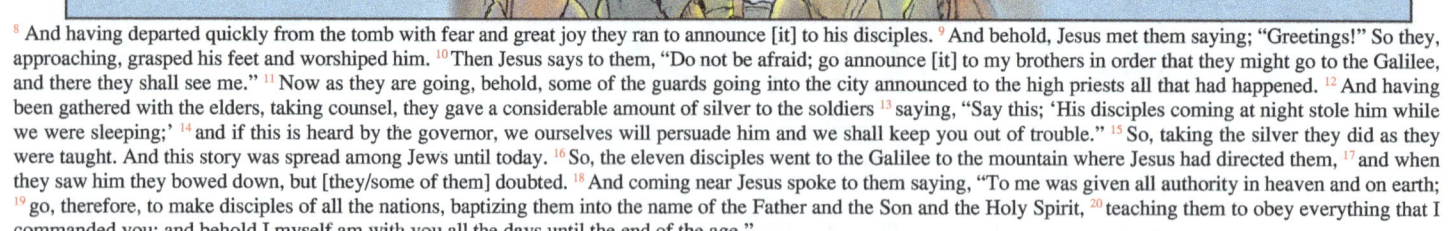

[8] And having departed quickly from the tomb with fear and great joy they ran to announce [it] to his disciples. [9] And behold, Jesus met them saying; "Greetings!" So they, approaching, grasped his feet and worshiped him. [10] Then Jesus says to them, "Do not be afraid; go announce [it] to my brothers in order that they might go to the Galilee, and there they shall see me." [11] Now as they are going, behold, some of the guards going into the city announced to the high priests all that had happened. [12] And having been gathered with the elders, taking counsel, they gave a considerable amount of silver to the soldiers [13] saying, "Say this; 'His disciples coming at night stole him while we were sleeping;' [14] and if this is heard by the governor, we ourselves will persuade him and we shall keep you out of trouble." [15] So, taking the silver they did as they were taught. And this story was spread among Jews until today. [16] So, the eleven disciples went to the Galilee to the mountain where Jesus had directed them, [17] and when they saw him they bowed down, but [they/some of them] doubted. [18] And coming near Jesus spoke to them saying, "To me was given all authority in heaven and on earth; [19] go, therefore, to make disciples of all the nations, baptizing them into the name of the Father and the Son and the Holy Spirit, [20] teaching them to obey everything that I commanded you; and behold I myself am with you all the days until the end of the age."

www.ingramcontent.com/pod-product-compliance
Lightning Source LLC
Chambersburg PA
CBHW080838230426
43665CB00021B/2886